A Devotional of Christian Encouragement and a Biblical Study About Grace and Healing for Those Facing Physical Hardship such as Chronic Pain or Illness, Depression, Imprisonment, Addiction, Cancer, or Recovering from Surgery.

EDWARD W. HELLMAN, M.D.

authorHOUSE®

AuthorHouse™
1663 Liberty Drive
Bloomington, IN 47403
www.authorhouse.com
Phone: 1 (800) 839-8640

© 2016 Edward W. Hellman, M.D. All rights reserved.

No part of this book may be reproduced, stored in a retrieval system, or transmitted by any means without the written permission of the author.

Unless otherwise mentioned in the text, all scriptural quotations were taken from the 1984 edition of The Holy Bible, New International Version, NIV, copyright 1973, 1978, 1984, 2011, by Biblica Inc.

Published by AuthorHouse   03/17/2016

ISBN: 978-1-5049-7358-8 (sc)
ISBN: 978-1-5049-7357-1 (hc)
ISBN: 978-1-5049-7359-5 (e)

Library of Congress Control Number: 2015920954

Print information available on the last page.

Any people depicted in stock imagery provided by Thinkstock are models, and such images are being used for illustrative purposes only. Certain stock imagery © Thinkstock.

This book is printed on acid-free paper.

Because of the dynamic nature of the Internet, any web addresses or links contained in this book may have changed since publication and may no longer be valid. The views expressed in this work are solely those of the author and do not necessarily reflect the views of the publisher, and the publisher hereby disclaims any responsibility for them.

May the words of my mouth and the meditation of my heart be pleasing in your sight, O Lord, my Rock and my Redeemer.
—Psalm 19:14

Search me, O God and know my heart; test me and know my thoughts. See if there is any offensive way in me, and lead me in the way everlasting.
—Psalm 139:23–24

I will sing to the Lord all my life; I will sing praise to my God as long as I live. May my meditation be pleasing to Him, as I rejoice in the Lord.
—Psalm 104:33–34

The Lord bless you and keep you; the Lord make His face shine upon you and be gracious to you; the Lord turn His face toward you and give you peace.
—Numbers 6:24–26

Dear friend, I pray that you may enjoy good health and that all may go well with you, even as your soul is getting along well.
—3 John 1:2

Arise, shine, for your light has come, and the glory of the Lord rises upon you.
—Isaiah 60:1

I pray that out of His glorious riches He may strengthen you with power through His Spirit in your inner being, so that Christ may dwell in your hearts through faith. And I pray that you, being rooted and established in love, may have power, together with all the saints, to grasp how wide and long and high and deep is the love of Christ, and to know this love that surpasses knowledge—that you may be filled to the measure of all the fullness of God.
—Ephesians 3:16–19

THE HOPE PROJECT

Do you not know? Have you not heard? The Lord is the everlasting God, the Creator of the ends of the earth. He will not grow tired or weary, and His understanding no one can fathom. He gives strength to the weary and increases the power of the weak. Even youths grow tired and weary, and young men stumble and fall; but those who hope in the Lord will renew their strength. They will soar on wings like eagles; they will run and not grow weary, they will walk and not be faint.

—Isaiah 40:28–31

I keep asking that the God of our Lord Jesus Christ, the glorious Father, may give you the Spirit of wisdom and revelation, so that you may know Him better. I pray also that the eyes of your heart may be enlightened in order that you may know the hope to which He has called you, the riches of His glorious inheritance in the saints, and His incomparably great power for us who believe. That power is like the working of His mighty strength, which He exerted in Christ when He raised Him from the dead and seated Him at His right hand in the heavenly realms, far above all rule and authority, power and dominion, and every title that can be given, not only in the present age but also in the one to come. And God placed all things under His feet and appointed Him to be head over everything for the church, which is His body, the fullness of Him who fills everything in every way.

—Ephesians 1:17–23

May the God of hope fill you with all joy and peace as you trust in Him, so that you may overflow with hope by the power of the Holy Spirit.

—Romans 15:13

May the God who gives endurance and encouragement give you a spirit of unity among yourselves as you follow Christ Jesus, so that with one heart and mouth you may glorify the God and Father of our Lord Jesus Christ.

—Romans 15:5–6

FOREWORD

I serve as the executive director for GraceWay Recovery Residence for women, located in Albany, Georgia. We treat women who have become addicted to drugs or alcohol, women with eating disorders, and even women who try to cut or otherwise injure themselves. As you might imagine, we do see a lot of hurt, loss, sadness, and discouragement in our ministry. But through encouragement, love, and showing them there is a better way, we have also seen how a life that seems broken can be radically changed. God's grace is more than enough to transform a life of hurt to one of victory.

This book is a breath of fresh air to those facing hardship. Part I is a forty-day devotional of scriptures particularly selected to offer hope and encouragement to anyone facing a difficulty. And don't we all face them to some degree? Who doesn't need encouragement? And what better place to get this than from our heavenly Father and His holy scripture? But it is more than that; providing encouragement to someone can literally put people on a path to having their very lives transformed by the grace of God. Part II is a biblical study looking at twelve principles from scripture that can help us to overcome any hardship that confronts us. What better resource to use for learning and growing in our walk than the book written by our Father who loves us and wants only the best for us?

I first met Dr. Hellman in 2005, when he, Paula Williams, and I came together to start a charity 5K run known as "Loop the Lake." Now in our tenth year, the run has raised thousands of dollars for women's charities. Through that time, I have come to know both Dr. Hellman and his wife, Emily, and we have become friends. We share the excitement that occurs when a person going through a hard time becomes transformed by the grace of God. Just as the 5K run is a project to provide support and encouragement to those going through hardship, so this book has a similar foundation. What we do as Christians is important, and one of the things

Edward W. Hellman, M.D.

we can do is to provide hope and encouragement to those going through adversity, sharing with them the message of God's grace and tender mercy. I congratulate Dr. Hellman on this book and am excited to see the ways God will use the scriptures in this book to encourage those facing difficulty.

My prayer is that the devotions in this book will prepare and nourish your soul with His daily bread to enlighten, comfort, and sustain you on your life journey, especially when the going gets tough.

The miracles of GraceWay and those of people facing a variety of hardships become evident as we surrender our wills and humbly purpose ourselves to cooperate with the gift of God's mercy and amazing grace. He desires to grant us serenity, truth, courage, wisdom, and humility to receive transformation in mind, body, and spirit. As He asks, "Do you want to be healed?" He waits patiently for our daily response. May the Almighty God, our Divine Physician, cleanse, prepare, and operate on your spirit as He performs soul surgery and heals you of your afflictions. This book is a remedy that will empower you to persevere, triumph, and give glory to the One who made you.

If you would like to learn more about GraceWay, please visit us at our website at www.gracewayrecovery.com. To learn or become involved in Loop the Lake, please visit us at www.loopthelake.com. We also have a ministry known as The Bread House, in which we make award-winning freshly milled whole grain and all-natural baked goods: wheat, artisan and sweet breads, cookies, granola, and fiber energy bars that can be shipped across the country from our website at www.thebreadhouse.com. Proceeds from The Bread House help support our ministry at GraceWay.

In God's grace,

Liz Dixon
Executive Director, GraceWay Recovery Residence

I love you, O Lord, my strength. The Lord is my rock, my fortress and my deliverer; my God is my rock, in whom I take refuge. He is my shield and the horn of my salvation, my stronghold. I call to the Lord, who is worthy of praise, and I am saved from my enemies.

The cords of death entangled me; the torrents of destruction overwhelmed me. The cords of the grave coiled around me; the snares of death confronted me. In my distress I called to the Lord; I cried to my God for help. From His temple He heard my voice; my cry came before Him, into His ears.

The earth trembled and quaked, and the foundations of the mountains shook; they trembled because He was angry. Smoke rose from His nostrils; consuming fire came from His mouth, burning coals blazed out of it. He parted the heavens and came down; dark clouds were under His feet. He mounted the cherubim and flew; He soared on the wings of the wind. He made darkness His covering, His canopy around Him—the dark rainclouds of the sky. Out of the brightness of His presence clouds advanced, with hailstones and bolts of lightning. The Lord thundered from heaven; the voice of the Most High resounded. He shot His arrows and scattered the enemies, great bolts of lightning and routed them. The valleys of the sea were exposed and the foundations of the earth laid bare at your rebuke, O Lord, at the blast of breath from your nostrils.

He reached down from on high and took hold of me; He drew me out of deep waters. He rescued me from my powerful enemy, from my foes, who were too strong for me. They confronted me in the day of my disaster, but the Lord was my support. He brought me out into a spacious place; He rescued me because He delighted in me …

You, O Lord, keep my lamp burning; my God turns my darkness into light. With your help I can advance against a troop, with my God I can scale a wall. As for God, His way is perfect; the word of the Lord is flawless. He is a shield for all who take refuge in Him. For who is God besides the Lord? And who is the Rock except our God? It is God who arms me with strength and makes my way perfect. He makes my feet like the feet of a

Edward W. Hellman, M.D.

deer; He enables me to stand on heights. He trains my hands for battle; my arms can bend a bow of bronze. You give me your shield of victory, and your right hand sustains me; you stoop down to make me great. You broaden the path beneath me, so that my ankles do not turn ...

The Lord lives! Praise be to my Rock! Exalted be God my Savior! ... Therefore I will praise you among the nations, O Lord; I will sing praises to your name. He gives His king great victories; He shows unfailing kindness to His anointed, to David and His descendants forever.
—Psalm 18:1-19, 28-36, 46, 49-50

ACKNOWLEDGMENTS

I truly have so many things to be thankful for that, if I were to write them down as words on paper, they would fill several volumes. What I can say is that they are written in my heart.

Thank you to God the Father, whose love for His only son, Jesus, is probably more than I can even fully appreciate, and yet He loved me enough to send Jesus to die for me so that I might be saved through Him. Just to think about how much God the Father must love Jesus, His only son, and yet to think He sent Him to redeem me is so incredibly humbling. Thank you also that He was so willing and generous to enter into a covenant relationship with us. Thank you to Jesus, who came down as God and flesh, knowing He was going to be brutally tortured and killed, all to redeem me from the wages of my sin, that whoever would call on the name of Jesus would be saved. Thank you to the Holy Spirit, who comes into each believer to counsel and empower us, helping us overcome anything that confronts us.

Thank you to my beautiful wife, Emily, whose outer beauty is only eclipsed by the beautiful person in Christ that she is on the inside. As I write this, my wife and I have just found out we are expecting our fifth child, and so to my children, Elijah, Joshua, Joy Anna, Isaiah, and Caleb, I am so thankful to God for the privilege of being your father and pray that I will be worthy of that very important calling. Thank you to my parents, Ann and Bill Hellman, and my in-laws, Anna and James Wynn, who have been such great role models for Emily and me in word but also in deed. Thank you to the rest of my family including my siblings and in-laws, Marty, Andrew, Tom, Kevin, Joe, Beth, Diane, Hannah, and Courtney; I am grateful for you all, and I pray we will all be drawn closer and closer to Jesus. Thank you to my church family, who has stood in the gap for me and my family and lifted us up in prayer and in so many other ways; and to the place of my spiritual rebirth, Sherwood Baptist Church, who

Edward W. Hellman, M.D.

continue to reach people throughout the world with their ministries, and my good friend there Jim McBride. Thank you to my partners Drs. Scott, Smith and Banks, my mid-levels Jimmy and Randy, my nurses Ricki and Kyra, my brothers and sisters at Georgia Sports and at New Covenant Church in Tifton. Thank you to Lawrence Thomas and his wife, April, a man and woman of true spiritual integrity. Thank you to the Reeds, who have become like family; to Dustin and Lindy Bengston who have done so much for our children and so many youth throughout Tifton through their swim program. Thank you to all the pastors and ministers who have sown so much into my family and me over the years.

I am thankful to my professional colleagues in the medical field with whom I serve as an orthopedic and spinal surgeon. I am grateful for the confidence that has been placed in me by so many specialists in medicine, such as other orthopedic surgeons and neurosurgeons, primary care doctors, therapists, rheumatologists, chiropractors, pain physicians, neurologists, and physiatrists, among others. They can, and do, choose to whom they send their patients, and I do not take lightly the privilege of serving them. There is an expression that it takes a village to raise a child, and it literally does take a "village" to produce a successful spinal surgery outcome in every single patient. I often get the credit, but there are so many more people involved that are truly unspoken heroes. From the orderlies that clean the operating rooms, to the nurses, medical doctors, and therapists that care for the patients, to my ever-so-patient assistants in surgery, to X-ray techs, to the anesthesia staff that "sleep" the patient, to the people that sterilize the equipment, to the students I have had the privilege to teach, the reps from implant companies we use, even to the administrators, case managers, and financial people that help run my practice and ensure we can have state-of-the-art equipment in surgery. All these are unspoken heroes in serving to provide excellence in spinal surgical outcomes, and I am so grateful. I see my spinal surgery practice as a ministry, an act of worship, and a platform to express the love of Jesus. I am totally committed to providing excellence in the spinal care of my patients because I feel like nothing short of excellence is worthy of our living God; you are all such a big part of it. Thank you so much for all you do!

Finally, to my patients and the people who are reading this book, thank you! What a privilege it is to serve you. You have truly become like family to me. We have laughed together and cried together. There are times when

I feel like I have served you really well, even miraculously so, but there are also times when I feel like I have failed you, and for that I apologize and ask for your forgiveness. In my heart, I earnestly hope and stand for being excellent in service to every patient I come in contact with. After sixteen years of being in practice and seeing about two hundred patients per week in the office and about four hundred cases per year in surgery, this amounts to about 160,000 patient visits and 6,400 surgeries on patients who have been placed in my care. I remember one time standing in a line at a church I was visiting, and the three people standing in front of me successively turned to me and told me how I had done surgery on them and how well they had done; I am embarrassed to say I did not fully recognize them. And yet, in those approximately 6,400 surgeries, there are patients who I felt like were arguably worse off than they were before they had surgery, and I can tell you almost to the most minute detail everything about them. In my busy office days, patients have passed through whom I know in retrospect I have failed to encourage, and people whom I have worked with or otherwise have been a part of my life that I have disappointed, and I am sorry for that. There is a part of the Bible about a shepherd losing one sheep in his care out of one hundred, and leaving the ninety-nine to find the one. I can identify with that verse, and I carry those people in particular whom I have in some way let down in my heart. But I know that in Christ, it is not over; He ultimately will restore all things. To my patients and people around me, then, I am grateful for you and the opportunity to serve you and pray in ever-increasing ways to be worthy of the calling I have received. In reading this book or in seeing me as a patient, I pray you will receive encouragement that will lead to hope, faith, love, and a healing in your life that is so miraculous that only Jesus could be behind it.

INTRODUCTION

And my God will meet all your needs according to His glorious riches in Christ Jesus.
—Philippians 4:19

I have told you these things, so that in me you may have peace. In this world you will have trouble. But take heart! I have overcome the world.
—John 16:33

For everything that was written in the past was written to teach us, so that through endurance and the encouragement of the Scriptures we might have hope.
—Romans 15:4

Have you ever experienced periods in your life when you feel like you are going through a storm? Instead of thriving, you feel like you are battling just to survive. You work hard to perform well at your job, but you get laid off; you do everything the doctor tells you to do, but your cancer returns; you try to do the right thing but end up getting punished for it. It can literally feel like you are on a boat being battered by wave after wave, with the fear of being capsized. You can feel afraid, even terrified—helpless, discouraged, overwhelmed, hopeless, abandoned, even frustrated or angry. You can feel very much alone and vulnerable when no one seems to understand what you are going through and there does not seem to be any help in sight. At that moment, you may even feel like God has forgotten about you or even abandoned you. I am here to tell you that we serve a great God. He is the alpha and the omega, the beginning and the end. He is all-powerful, and through Him all things were made. No one can open a door

Edward W. Hellman, M.D.

He has shut, or shut a door He has opened. He is ever present; He is with you but also goes before you. He loves you and created you in His likeness and image; He knows even the very number of hairs on your head. He wants you to be joyful and live in victory even to the point that He sent His one and only son, Jesus, to come and die for you so you would be enabled to do so. He has given you the right to call Him Dad, and you are therefore a child of the Most High God.

There was a man named Peter who found himself in such a storm. He had followed Jesus onto a boat, and a storm came up that was so furious that waves were coming up over the sides. It must have appeared as if the entire boat was going to capsize, and Peter was afraid. In the end, Jesus was with him and rebuked the winds and the waves, calming the storm and getting them to where they were going. "It is I. Take courage. Do not be afraid," said Jesus to His apostles in another storm. He wants us to know He is with us and we have nothing to fear, even in the very storms of life that you may be facing. He will never leave you or forsake you. He wants you to have victory and share His message of salvation with others, acting as His ambassadors and as His body here on earth.

In some ways, each of us is a pastor, and the sermons we preach include not only the words we speak but how we live our very lives. The words we say, the things we do, and how we treat people can have a lasting effect on those we meet. We are like farmers who sow seeds in the soil; the harvest and the fruit that is produced become our legacy, a measurement of our impact on the world for generations to come. The Bible talks about the sowing of "good seed" and "bad seed" and how, at the Day of Judgment, the harvest will occur and the good and bad crops separated. We sow seed in so many ways. Some of it may seem big, such as raising children, and some may seem small, such as a single kind act for a stranger you may never see again, but none of these seeds are insignificant. Each can grow and produce an amazing crop that goes on to make more and more seeds, or it can produce a crop of thorns and bristles.

Edward Kimball was a Sunday school teacher who shared the love of Christ with a young man with a 5th grade education selling shoes in a store on April 21st, 1855; on the surface, seemingly not a big deal. The man's name was D. L. Moody who became so passionate about Jesus that he ultimately started the Moody Bible Institute, which has graduated thousands of students and has impacted millions of people throughout the world for Christ. Mr. Moody also befriended and worked with a man named J. Wilbur Chapman, who then went on to work with a man named Billy Sunday, who led a meeting in Charlotte, North Carolina that inspired the formation of a men's group there that later invited a preacher named Mordecai Ham to do an evangelical crusade in Charlotte. It was at this crusade on November 1st, 1934 that a nearly 16 year-old boy accepted Christ whose name turned out to be Billy Graham. I read one account that an estimated 2.2 billion people throughout the world have heard Billy Graham preach about Jesus. In 1949, at a Billy Graham crusade, a man named Louis Zamperini gave his life to Christ. He was a former Olympian who fought in World War II and was taken a prisoner of war in Japan and cruelly treated. When he returned home, he slipped into a world of alcohol and post-traumatic stress. But, because of his conversion at the crusade, he was able to turn his life around and return to Japan to forgive his former captors. As I write this, the movie Unbroken featuring the story of Louis Zamperini was just released, inspiring millions. Isn't it amazing what God can do with one seemingly small seed planted in 1855, an obedient heart, and it is still producing fruit even today? God is so good, and his word is so powerful!

We also have many roles in our lives. I am a husband, a father, a son, an uncle, a cousin, a friend, a stranger, a colleague, a surgeon, and a boss, to name a few. My hope is that in each of these roles I will sow seeds that will build people up and encourage them and point them to Jesus. One of the areas I serve is in the field of orthopedic and spinal surgery, and it is such a privilege. On office days, my mid-levels and I may see upward of ninety to one hundred patients in a single day. Most of my patients are going through a hardship of one form or another. It may be from an injury, it may be from an arthritic condition or deformity, but they are usually going through some form of physical suffering. I can testify that there is a lot of physical suffering and hardship that a person can experience in his or her lifetime. But I can also testify that where pain and suffering may abound, God's grace and blessings abound even more. This book is intended to be a way to sow seeds of hope and encouragement to those who are going through a hard time. The grace and love of Jesus is more than enough to overcome anything that confronts you. Through Him, we are more than conquerors.

Thank you so much for taking the time to read this. What a privilege and blessing to have you here! My prayer is that in reading this, you will be greatly encouraged and that the encouragement you receive will be a blessing to you but also that it will be so overflowing that it will flow out of

Edward W. Hellman, M.D.

you to others, so that they may reap a blessing as well. The encouragement we receive from God and his scripture can do that. God wants to bless us, and He has blessed us, and by being blessed, I believe He wants us to share this blessing with others as well; as Jesus said, "If anyone is thirsty, let him come to me and drink. Whoever believes in me, as the scripture has said, streams of living water will flow from within him" (John 7:37-38). Put another way with regards to encouraging someone going through hardship, "Praise be to the God and Father of our Lord Jesus Christ, the Father of compassion and the God of all comfort, who comforts us in all our troubles, so that we can comfort those in any trouble with the comfort we ourselves have received from God. For just as the sufferings of Christ flow over into our lives, so also through Christ our comfort overflows. If we are distressed, it is for your comfort and salvation; if we are comforted, it is for your comfort, which produces in you patient endurance in the same sufferings we suffer. And our hope for you is firm, because we know that just as you share in our sufferings, so also you share in our comfort" (2 Corinthians 1:3-7). How encouraging! Where sufferings flow into our lives, through Christ, comfort overflows! God's grace is more than sufficient for whatever confronts us.

It is so important to be a voice that offers hope to believers and unbelievers alike, carrying a message to show there really is a better way. Jesus offers this encouragement in John 16:33: "I have told you these things, so that in me you may have peace. In this world you will have trouble. But take heart! I have overcome the world." When you consider this with the famous scripture of John 3:16, "For God so loved the world that He sent His one and only Son, that whoever believes in Him may not perish but have eternal life," we can appreciate that He overcame the world for us. Jesus wants us to be encouraged (take heart!). He wants us to understand that in Him you may have peace, even in a world full of troubles. Jesus has already paid the price, He has already won the battle, and the victory is already ours. For a Christian to walk in victory today is simply to walk on ground that has already been conquered. In fact, when people asked Jesus, "What must we do to do the works that God requires?" Jesus answered simply this: "The work of God is this: to believe in the one He has sent" (John 6:29). That was it. Not a long list of things we must do or accomplish before we die. The importance of John 16:33 in encouraging His disciples is not only in the words themselves but also in the timing of the verse itself. It is the last verse recorded in the book of John before Jesus prays for Himself, His disciples, and all believers, right before Judas betrays him into the hands of the mob. If you were going to say one last important thing to your followers, this would be the time. Jesus takes this time to encourage His followers. Jesus warns them that those in the world will have trouble but tells them to be encouraged because He has overcome the world and those in Him can have peace. That message is not just for his disciples back then. I believe it is just as important a message for His followers today: "I have told you these things so that in me you may have peace. In this world you will have trouble. But take heart! I have overcome the world." Why is that so important? The Bible actually represents a sacred covenant that God has made with us, made in blood and eternally binding. I will discuss this later in the book, but Jesus is actually the critical part of that covenant; those who believe in Him are literally in Him. So if Jesus says He has overcome the world, and those who believe in Him are in Him, then we too have overcome the world (through Jesus) as participants with God in this sacred and powerful covenant.

There is an enormous spiritual battle all around us, of which most of us are largely unaware. The Bible speaks of it. I am not talking about the battle determining the ultimate outcome of God versus Satan. That battle was won a long time ago when Jesus redeemed us and won victory over sin and death, offering us eternal life with Him in heaven. What I am talking about is the battle that involves your day-to-day life here and now. The Bible says Jesus came that you may have life and have it more abundantly, but that "the thief" comes only to steal, kill, and destroy; he has been defeated eternally, but that does not keep him from going after you, your family, and everyone you know right now. He is known as a deceiver, liar, and accuser. He would like nothing more than to keep you discouraged, fearful, feeling guilty, living in failure, and bearing little if any fruit. But that is not your destiny; that is not what you were intended for. The old Sunday school story tells of the egg that fell out of an eagle's nest and landed in a chicken coop. The young eagle did not know any better and grew up scratching the dirt and eating the small amount of corn that was thrown to him each day with the chickens. He did not even realize he could easily fly out of the coop. One day he saw an eagle soaring in the sky and wished he could be like that eagle. Shortly after that, he learned his true identity and claimed his destiny of flying in the air with the other eagles. You are a son or daughter of the Most High God. It is not your destiny to live in shame, or guilt, or failure, or to live in any way short of complete and total victory. To believe

Edward W. Hellman, M.D.

anything else is to believe the lies of Satan. This battle I am talking about, then, is the battle over the beliefs and actions that make up your day-to-day life. Are you walking in victory? You should be! It is your destiny. What is your armor to fight and win this battle? Read this:

> Finally, be strong in the Lord and his mighty power. Put on the full armor of God so that you can take your stand against the devil's schemes. For our struggle is not against flesh and blood, but against the rulers, against the authorities, against the powers of this dark world and against the spiritual forces of evil in the heavenly realms. Therefore put on the full armor of God, so that when the day of evil comes, you may be able to stand your ground, and after you have done everything, to stand. Stand firm then, with the belt of truth buckled around your waist, with the breastplate of righteousness in place, and with your feet fitted with the readiness that comes from the gospel of peace. In addition to all this, take up the shield of faith, with which you can extinguish all the flaming arrows of the evil one. Take the helmet of salvation and the sword of the Spirit, which is the word of God. (Ephesians 6:10–17)

Can you imagine being in a fight and having at your disposal only things to defend yourself but no offensive weapons? I guess you could hope to tire the other person out as he struck you over and over, but it would be hard to put much of a hurt on your foe. Notice that the word of God is the sword of the Spirit and the only offensive weapon mentioned to use in this spiritual battle. From a spiritual battle perspective, this book is filled with scripture to try to encourage those who are going through hardship and may have lost some hope. Take heart! Be encouraged! In Christ you are more than a conqueror! Fill your daily thoughts with His scriptures of encouragement. Learn the scripture's amazing promises for you and claim them for your life. Put on your armor, grab your sword, and suit up! It is game on!

    I see this book as an extension of my practice. My hope is to be excellent in service as an orthopedic and spinal surgeon to my patients, such that my practice will serve as a platform and testimony to the greatness of God. He deserves our very best. In pursuing excellence, my desire is for this to be a source of encouragement to my patients going through hardship and that this experience will draw them closer to Jesus. In a similar fashion, this book is written for anyone going through a physical hardship, whether it is from chronic pain, illness, imprisonment, cancer, depression, or in recovery from surgery. My hope is that in reading this, people will be encouraged and draw closer to Jesus through the holy scriptures.

The book is divided into two sections. Part I is a forty-day devotional containing scriptures I believe provide encouragement for someone going through physical hardship. You may have a tendency to want to jump ahead in this devotional, but I would encourage you to take one scripture, one day at a time and really think about it, pray for understanding, and internalize it. Carry it in your heart as you go through the day. You may notice that beyond the scripture, my comments in the devotional are pretty brief; there is simply not much I can add beyond my appreciation for what that individual scripture may mean to me, and it may not mean the same thing to you. The second part is a section that discusses biblical instruction to people going through hardship. I really believe that among the many functions of the Bible is that it is an underused and underappreciated "owner's manual" to use for our lives and for overcoming anything that faces us. Even more than that—and I will discuss this idea in more detail later in this book—the holy scripture represents a sacred covenant that God has made with us. He has entered into a covenant relationship with us, and the Bible literally describes in great detail the nature of this great and generous inheritance He has given us. Imagine having a wealthy relative and hearing he has given you a precious gift. Wouldn't you be excited to see what it is? The resources and gifts that are there in the Bible waiting for you are incredible. Scripture is not only a source of encouragement but also a source itself of great healing power, as I discuss later in this book as well. My prayer is that in reading this book you will be blessed and encouraged in ever-increasing measure to more than overcome anything that confronts you.

Enjoy! Be blessed!

Edward W. Hellman, M.D.

Part 1

DEVOTIONAL

Let us hold unswervingly to the hope we profess, for He who promised is faithful. And let us consider how we may spur one another on toward love and good deeds. Let us not give up meeting together, as some are in the habit of doing, but let us encourage one another—and all the more as you see the Day approaching.

—Hebrews 10:23–25

Day 1

> The Lord your God is with you, He is mighty to save. He will take great delight in you, He will quiet you with His love, He will rejoice over you with singing.
> —Zephaniah 3:17

Since becoming a father of now five children under the age of eight, this scripture has taken on so much new meaning to me. In my own way, I know what it is to delight in my children; I carry a picture of my family in my lab coat and show it to just about everyone I come in contact with—sometimes even to complete strangers. When I start talking or thinking about my children, I get such a feeling of complete joy in my spirit. I also know what it is to quiet them with love. If they fall and get hurt or if they are going through something hard, I want to wrap them in my arms and quiet them with my love; when they succeed, I rejoice over them and with them with singing.

It is amazing to think about, but scripture testifies to its truth. The all-powerful God who created the universe and everything in it and who is truly mighty to save takes great delight in you. And when you go through something hard, He is standing there waiting to quiet you with His perfect love and to rejoice over you with His singing. In scripture, Jesus actually says, "I will declare your name to my brothers; in the presence of the congregation I will sing your praises" (Hebrews 2:12). Imagine Him up in heaven bragging to anyone who will listen about how great you are and how much He loves you—or how He loves it when you turn to Him in a time of distress for His help and love. Imagine Him saying how He appreciates it when you turn to Him with thanks during your good times, so He can rejoice over you with singing.

If I know how it is to delight in my children, to quiet them with my love during their hard times, or to rejoice over them with singing, how much more is God willing and able to do that for us!

Thank You, Lord, that You are mighty and yet delight in us. Thank You, Lord, that You are there to quiet us with Your love during hard times and that You rejoice over us with singing!

Day 2

> For I am convinced that neither death nor life, neither angels nor demons, neither the present nor the future, nor any powers, neither height nor depth, nor anything else in all creation, will be able to separate us from the love of God that is in Christ Jesus our Lord.
>
> —Romans 8:38-39

To a person going through physical hardship, the term "nothing" can have a lot of negative connotations. You may have been told by doctors that they have nothing to offer you. You may feel so worn out, like you have nothing left. On your particularly hard days, you may feel like "a nothing." But consider this: there is the great and powerful love of God, and there is nothing that can ever keep you from access to it. That bears repeating—there is nothing in all creation that can separate you from God's love. The interesting thing to think about is this: that "nothing" includes you! Even you cannot separate yourself from God's love! On your worst day, when you may have acted in a way you now regret or said something you wish you hadn't—or even completely rejected God—He still loves you. His love is not dependent on your actions. The Bible says He is faithful even when you are not. How is that for a "nothing"? If you feel yourself beginning to think negatively, think about how great God's love is and that there is nothing in all creation that can separate you from it! Nothing!

Thank You, Lord, that You love us like You do and that You are so faithful in Your love. Thank You that nothing exists that can separate us from Your love—not even ourselves.

Day 3

> Do you not know? Have you not heard? The Lord is the everlasting God, the Creator of the ends of the earth. He will not grow tired or weary, and His understanding no one can fathom. He gives strength to the weary and increases the power of the weak. Even youths grow tired and weary, and young men stumble and fall; but those who hope in the Lord will renew their strength. They will soar on wings like eagles; they will run and not grow weary, they will walk and not be faint.
>
> —Isaiah 40:28–31

It may be something you have not contemplated lately. You may have taken some of your focus off God and placed it on the doctor sitting in front of you. And not only that, the doctor may have told you something that was not very good. But be encouraged that our God is a magnificent God. He is powerful, He is holy, and His ways are perfect; His love is perfect, and He loves you. He really, really, *really* loves you. He is capable. Try placing your hope in the Lord—not as a last resort but as a first resort and as a privilege and an opportunity. Hope in the Lord, and you will never be disappointed—you will never be shamed. He is so worthy, and He wants to help you. Hope in Him. Various Bible translations will either use the word *hope* or *wait* in this scripture, but it is interesting to note that the original word in Hebrew קָוָה (*qavah*) is not easily translated into English. It actually carries a similar meaning to "braiding together," as in making a cord. So when we "braid ourselves together" with God, as has already been done in our covenant with Him, all these good things mentioned above will happen.

Thank You, Lord, that You are our God. You are mighty, and You do not grow weary or tired. Your wisdom and knowledge no one can fathom. And yet You are so compassionate and loving to us. You see us grow weary and stumble, and in Your mercy and love, You reach down and help and strengthen us. You are the God Almighty (El Shaddai), the God who sees me (El Roi), and the God who provides (Yahweh Yireh). Thank You, Lord!

Day 4

> "For I know the plans I have for you," declares the Lord, "plans to prosper you and not to harm you, plans to give you hope and a future. Then you will call upon me and come and pray to me, and I will listen to you. You will seek me and find me when you seek me with all your heart."
>
> —Jeremiah 29:11–13

You are not an accident. You are not the outcome of an evolutionary process in which you developed from an amoeba. You are a child of the Most High God, and God has a plan for your life! These plans include spiritual and physical prosperity, a future, and absolutely no harm. Maybe you think that God's plans are for someone else or are just for people in general but not necessarily for you; or maybe you think the promises in the Bible have somehow expired, like a carton of old milk. It bears repeating that God says He knows the plans He has for you. HIs plans are designed to prosper you and to give you hope and a future—and to never harm you. The Bible says, "But the plans of the Lord stand firm forever, the purposes of His heart through all generations" (Psalm 33:11).

Take comfort that no matter what you are going through right now, the God who made the entire universe and everything in it has a wonderful plan for your life.

Lord, thank You that You have a wonderful plan for my life, and thank You that this plan involves prosperity, hope, and a future—and absolutely no harm. Lord, even if I don't fully understand why I am going through what I am going through right now, know that I appreciate that You have a plan for my life and that I want to follow it. Thank You.

Day 5

> Hear, O Israel, today you are going into battle against your enemies. Do not be fainthearted or afraid; do not be terrified or give way to panic before them. For the Lord your God is the one who goes with you to fight for you against your enemies to give you victory.
>
> —Deuteronomy 20:3-4

If you have the chance to read the next part of this chapter in Deuteronomy, it is interesting to note how the Bible basically instructs the leaders of the army to send home any of the soldiers who were recently married, had recently built a home, had recently planted a vineyard, or were just fainthearted or afraid. Basically, just about anyone who did not want to be in the army was allowed to go home and even encouraged to do so—despite the general idea that the army of Israel seems to be usually outnumbered to begin with. The story of Gideon and his army was a dramatic example of this. Gideon faced an army of 135,000 Philistine soldiers with about 32,000 of his own men. They were outnumbered about four to one. What did God do? He had Gideon keep sending men home until they got down to an army of three hundred men! So they went from being outnumbered four to one to being outnumbered over four hundred to one! But those who stayed were courageous and obedient to God, and they routed and destroyed the much larger army.

Do you ever feel like you are heading into a battle? Or that maybe every day seems like a battle? Or worse, do you feel like you are in a battle and were counting on help from some people who have suddenly deserted you? Maybe you feel like the odds are stacked against you. Can I tell you something? God is there with you, and He has already promised to give you victory. He is all you need. The battle is His, and the victory will be yours. What do you have to do? Don't be afraid, don't panic, don't even be fainthearted. Be still! "Be still and know that I am God" (Psalm 46:10); and, "The Lord will fight for you; you need only to be still" (Exodus 14:14).

Thank You, Lord, that You go into our battles with us and give us victory no matter what the odds are. Thank You, Lord!

Day 6

> The Lord is my shepherd, I shall not be in want. He makes me lie down in green pastures, He leads me beside quiet waters, He restores my soul. He guides me in paths of righteousness for His name's sake. Even though I walk through the valley of the shadow of death, I will fear no evil, for you are with me; your rod and your staff, they comfort me. You prepare a table before me in the presence of my enemies. You anoint my head with oil; my cup overflows. Surely goodness and love will follow me all the days of my life, and I will dwell in the house of the Lord forever.
> —Psalm 23

What a beautiful and encouraging psalm! You may be going through a really hard time right now. If great times can be compared to mountain peaks and bad times to valleys, you might feel like you are truly in a really deep valley right now. I do not in any way want to minimize the hardship you are going through, but take comfort in knowing that Christ has already defeated death. The Bible says, "Death has been swallowed up in victory" (1 Corinthians 15:55). What you see all around you may seem like a valley of death, but know that it is not real; it is simply a shadow and a lie. A shadow is simply a lack of light, nothing else. And do you know what? Through it all, Jesus is right there by your side. He is the light of the world and can eliminate any shadow and show it for what it is. A shadow cannot overcome light. Deception cannot overcome the truth. The truth is that you are anointed! Goodness and love will follow you every day of your life! Your future is to dwell in the house of the Lord forever. What could possibly be better than that?

Thank You, Lord, that You are my good shepherd, watching over me, guiding and protecting me. Thank You that You are the light of the world and Your light destroys the shadows of deception. Thank You that in You I have received an anointing, and that in You my soul is restored. Thank You that You have already defeated death, and that what I may see as death is only a shadow and a lie. Thank You that You walk through these valleys of hard times with me; thank You that goodness and love will follow me all the days of my life and that my future is to dwell in Your house forever. Thank You!

Day 7

> By His wounds we are healed.
>
> —Isaiah 53:5

> By His wounds you have been healed.
>
> —1 Peter 2:24

The Book of Isaiah is pretty amazing to me. It was written about seven hundred years before the birth of Jesus, and yet it contains approximately twenty prophecies about the life of Jesus, the Messiah, including that he would be born of a virgin, have a ministry in Galilee, be rejected by many, suffer, and even be buried in a rich man's tomb. Isaiah 53:5 talks about the idea that when the Messiah comes, we will be healed by his wounds, and there is a verse in 1 Peter 2:24 that on the surface sounds just like it: "By his wounds you have been healed." There is one important difference between the verse in Isaiah and the verse in Peter from which we can take great comfort and encouragement. Notice that in Peter it says that we *have been* healed, as in the past tense. What should that mean to us? It means that any work that needs to be done for you to be healed has already been done! What did Jesus say on the cross? "It is finished" (John 19:30). And at that point, every work that ever needed to be done for you to live in total victory and be healed from any sickness was completed.

Do not misunderstand me. If you are seeing a doctor and, through a course of evaluation and treatment for a condition you have, the doctor and you have come up with a reasonable plan for your treatment, I am not saying you should not do it. What I am saying is that about two thousand years ago, Jesus came down as God in the flesh and took all of our sickness, transgressions, and even death on his shoulders and paid the ultimate price for you to be healed of them. Understand that healing from your condition is your God-given right as a son or daughter of God and that any work that needed to be done for this to occur was done a long time ago on the cross. There is simply no more work left to be done. Understand this and claim it for your life. Meditate on it, take it into your heart, and really internalize

Edward W. Hellman, M.D.

it. Not to claim this truth for your life is to reject one of the biggest gifts Jesus has given us.

Lord Jesus, thank You that You did come down to earth to redeem us from sickness and death. Scripture in Isaiah said You would be beaten and suffer, even to the point that You were not recognizable as a human being. You knew this ahead of time and still came for us. Thank You for your incredible love and sacrifice, that by Your wounds we *were* truly healed.

Day 8

> And we know that in all things God works for the good of those
> who love Him, who have been called according to His purpose.
> —Romans 8:28

You may be going through some incredibly hard times right now. You might understandably be discouraged; you might have even lost hope of things ever getting better. Please know that God loves you and also that no matter what your current situation is, no matter how bad or hopeless it may seem, God can meet you there and work it for your good. Romans 8:28 says that in *all* things (not some things), God will work for the good of those who love Him.

The Bible tells the story of the prodigal son in the book of Luke. The son had basically abandoned his family, taken his inheritance, squandered it in a foreign land, and rejected his father and everything he had been taught and raised to be. But when the son was out of money, even starving, he returned to his father, really just with the hope that his father would take him back as a servant so that he could at least get something to eat and survive. But the part of the story I love is that the Bible says that when the son "was still a long way off," his father saw him and ran to him and embraced him; remarkably, he restored his rights as a son to him. His father had been watching out for him! God is like that. You might feel like you are in a really bad place. You might have even turned your back on God. You might even feel like you do not deserve God, but God is watching you and longs for you to turn to Him. He will meet you at whatever place you are, even run to you and embrace you. He loves you. The Bible even talks about the rejoicing that occurs in heaven when someone turns their ways back to God. What an awesome thought.

Thank You, Lord, that no matter where I am, no matter what I am going through, even no matter what I may have done, You will meet me in my time of need and work for my good. Thank You for all the times before that You have met me in my need and worked on my behalf. Thank You that You will work in any and every situation I find myself in and turn it around for my good. Thank You. I love You, God.

Day 9

> Do not let your hearts be troubled. Trust in God; trust also in me. In my Father's house are many rooms. If that were not so, I would have told you. I am going there to prepare a place for you. And if I go and prepare a place for you, I will come back and take you to be with me that you may also be where I am. You know the way to the place I am going.
>
> —John 14:1-4

Some people may spend a majority of their waking hours working at a job they do not like or find fulfillment in at all. Sometimes the only thing that will keep them going, even for years on end, is their plan for retirement. If they can just put enough money in their 401(k), or work long enough to get a certain pension, they will retire and finally be able to enjoy life. They will often put up with a lot of bad times just with the hope that things will get better in the future. John 14 talks about the ultimate retirement plan. What could be better than knowing Jesus not only came down and redeemed us from sin and death but also that when He ascended up to heaven, He went to prepare a place for us? For those of us going through hard times, Jesus says, "Do not let your hearts be troubled." Things are about to get a lot better! I have not read a lot of books about life-after-death experiences, but I did read *Ninety Minutes in Heaven* and *Heaven Is for Real*, and it is exciting to me to think about what heaven is like and how great it must be. When you are going through particularly hard times, please think about Jesus up in heaven preparing a place for you and Him coming back and taking you there and how amazing that will be. The Bible actually says, "No eye has seen, no ear has heard, no mind has conceived what God has prepared for those who love Him" (1 Corinthians 2:9). Wow!

Thank You, God, that when You went up to heaven, You went to prepare a place for me. Thank You that You have promised to come back for me and take me there. Thank You, Lord; I believe and trust and stand on Your promises and am excited to go at some point in Your timing to the place You have prepared for me. Thank You, Lord!

Day 10

> So do not fear, for I am with you; do not be dismayed, for I am your God. I will strengthen you and help you; I will uphold you with my righteous right hand. All who rage against you will surely be ashamed and disgraced; those who oppose you will be as nothing and perish. Though you search for your enemies, you will not find them. Those who wage war against you will be as nothing at all. For I am the Lord, your God, who takes hold of your right hand and says to you; do not fear; I will help you.
> —Isaiah 41:10-13

The news you have been hearing lately may not have been too good. You may feel like the things and people you thought you could rely on have failed you. You may be frustrated, hurt, hopeless, or just plain afraid about what confronts you. You may have been told you have cancer, a terminal neurologic condition, or (perhaps worse) that all your tests were normal and that no explanation could be found for the problems you are experiencing. Traditional medicine may have led to numerous tests and exhaustive treatments but no cure or even improvement in your condition. In all this, our great God, Jehovah Rapha (God the Healer), reaches down and encourages us; do not fear, do not be dismayed. God is with you and has you by the hand and will strengthen you. Even when all else fails and your situation may seem hopeless, God promises He is there and will help you. The next time you are confronted by something that threatens to overcome you, imagine your great and powerful God standing right beside you and holding your hand, like a big brother who follows you wherever you go but so much better. Claim the promise of God for your life that He will be with you and strengthen and help you and destroy all your enemies who oppose you.

Thank You, God, that You are great and powerful but that You are also ever present. You are not a God who keeps His distance from me. Thank You that You have promised to take me by my hand and strengthen and help me. Thank You, Lord!

Day 11

> Come to me, all you who are weary and burdened, and I will give you rest. Take my yoke upon you and learn from me, for I am gentle and humble in heart, and you will find rest for your souls. For my yoke is easy and my burden is light.
> —Matthew 11:28–30

To me, there is a difference between being simply tired and being weary. I love to work hard. When I am off, this usually involves going out and working in the yard, going to bed tired and getting a great night's rest, and waking up and feeling so refreshed in the morning; it is such a simple pleasure. Being weary and burdened is different than that and is something I think to varying degrees we have all experienced. We go to bed at night exhausted, we toss and turn all night thinking about the many problems we face or all the things that have gone wrong, and when we wake up, we are still exhausted, possibly dreading the day ahead and what we think it may hold. No amount of time in bed can cure being weary.

If you are weary and burdened, God invites you to come to Him. He wants to have a relationship with you and show you a better way. He wants to show you the way to find rest for your soul. Imagine the God over the entire world and its billions of people and their billions of problems, yet He says His yoke is easy and His burden is light. He wants you to be refreshed. Notice in this verse He does not say He is going to take you out of the place you are in to a place where you are never confronted with any sort of problem, but rather that He will teach you how to find rest for your soul, even in your environment of trials and tribulations.

Thank You, Lord, that You have invited us to come to You, not asking that we come to You only when we are in a state of peace and calm; rather, You have invited us to come to You when we are weary and burdened. Thank You that You have a gentle and humble heart and that You will teach us a way to find true rest for our souls, no matter what we are going through. Thank You that You are so willing to help. Thank You, Lord.

Day 12

> For God so loved the world that He gave His one and only Son,
> that whoever believes in Him shall not perish but have eternal life.
> —John 3:16

Think about something you really love, no matter what it is. Think about how perfect God is and so how strong His love must be. The Bible says Jesus was God's one and only Son. God the Father must really, really love Jesus, even to a point we cannot really fully appreciate or even comprehend. For me, the love I have for my family gives me the smallest appreciation for how great God's love for Jesus must be. Yet God loves you also, and He loves you a lot. He is a father who will do just about anything to help you. He will hold nothing back nor leave any stone unturned to help you in your time of need and distress. If you believe in Jesus and what He did for you, you have been given the gift of eternal life.

Around military holidays, we often hear that freedom is not free. Is that not so true? There are and have been people throughout the history of our nation who have put themselves in harm's way to protect our freedom. Many have even died doing so, making the ultimate sacrifice. Our spiritual freedom is not free, either. Jesus paid the ultimate price and redeemed us from sin and death by dying on the cross. Our freedom was bought with a price but is offered as a gift to us. If you are going through a hardship of one form or another, do not forget there is a God who loves you so much He holds nothing back. He sent His one and only son to die for you and redeem you so that if you believe in Him, you may have eternal life.

"If God is for us, who can be against us? He who did not spare His own Son, but gave Him up for us all—how will He not also, along with Him, graciously give us all things?" (Romans 8:31-32).

Thank You, Lord, that You do love us. Thank You, Lord, that You are not distant and uncaring. You are ever-present and loving and compassionate and merciful. Thank You that You have held nothing back from us, even Your most precious son, Jesus. Thank You, God, for Jesus and that You love us like you do.

Day 13

With God, all things are possible.

—Matthew 19:26

If you are going through hard times, it is likely that this message in Matthew completely contradicts everything you have been told or even believed about your current situation. You may have been told that you are sick, that no treatment is likely to succeed, or even that your case is terminal. You may have been left with a feeling of discouragement and hopelessness. But please understand this: with God, *all* things are possible.

To me, our spiritual lives are much more like the sport of tennis than football. In football, a team can have developed such a large lead going into the fourth quarter that even if the losing team plays perfectly in the last quarter, they will probably still lose the game, simply because they are so far behind. That is why it is not uncommon to see fans leaving football games early (as well as in baseball and basketball), because the outcome of the game might be decided well before the actual game ends. Tennis is not like that. The person who wins the match is the person who has won the very last point. Even if a tennis player is being badly beaten and down to even the last point, if he can collect himself, not give up, and start winning points, he can completely reverse his fate and win the match. You may have gone through some horrible times and felt like you have been beaten down and defeated over and over, and even that there is no chance you will ever walk in victory. But remember that with God, *all* things are possible. The game is not over! That includes you and your present situation, no matter how hopeless it may seem to you or how late in the game you may be. There is simply nothing too hard for God to handle. Have you invited Him in to be with you in your current situation? If you have, be encouraged that nothing is impossible with Him. As long as you have a breath in you, it is never too late. It is not over.

Thank You, Lord, that You are a great and all-powerful God and that all things are possible with You. There is nothing about my current situation, no matter how hopeless it may seem to me, that is impossible or even hard for You to fix. Thank You, Lord, that You are with us and *all* things are possible with You!

Day 14

> The Lord Himself goes before you and will be with you; He will never leave you nor forsake you. Do not be afraid; do not be discouraged.
> —Deuteronomy 31:8

Sometimes things are so clear and predictable that you can see them coming well before they occur, but sometimes they are not. Who expects their house to burn down, or their company to "move in another direction," or the biopsy to come back positive? Life can really throw things at us—sometimes good and sometimes not so good, sometime anticipated and sometimes not so much. When things are going along pretty well and something really big and unexpected and really bad happens to you, it can feel like you just got punched in the stomach. There can actually be physical pain associated with stressful situations, and physiologic changes can occur in your body. In medicine, this is known as a fight-or-flight response, which literally feels like you are running or fighting for your very survival. Please take comfort in knowing that whatever you have suddenly come upon, "the Lord himself goes before you." He is beside you but also in front of you. The situation you are facing has already been seen and handled by God. Nothing surprises God, and certainly there is nothing He cannot handle. He goes before you; He will be with you; He will never leave you; He will never forsake you. His advice: "Do not be afraid, do not be discouraged." Or, as I saw on a T-shirt yesterday at a Christian bookstore: "I got it. —God."

Thank You, Lord, that You do have it: that You go before us, that You are with us, and that You will never leave or forsake us. Thank You, Lord, that there is nothing we will ever come upon that surprises You or that You have not already seen and taken care of for us. Thank You, Lord.

Day 15

> Isn't this the carpenter?
>
> —Mark 6:3

There are over two hundred names used in the Bible to describe Jesus. He is called the Redeemer, the Advocate, the Lamb of God, the Amen, the Way, the Truth, the Life, the Author and Finisher of our faith, the Good Shepherd, the Gate, the Beloved Son, the Branch, the Vine, the Cornerstone, the Bread of Life, among many other titles. Before He began His ministry at the age of thirty, He was a carpenter. His identity was so wrapped up in being a carpenter that when Jesus first returned home to preach, the villagers said, "Isn't this the carpenter?" and they took offense at Him. Even His own brothers did not initially believe He was the Messiah.

I find it encouraging to think of Jesus, our Lord and Savior, being a carpenter. I am an orthopedic surgeon, and orthopedic surgeons are basically carpenters who work on the human body. Carpenters fix and build things; they tend to be practical and hardworking; their hands are strong and calloused. If I ever needed help with something, I would turn to a carpenter. If I were looking for help with something and had to pick from a group of a hundred people I did not know, I would shake their hands, and the one with the most calloused, strong, even beaten-up pair of hands would be the one I would pick. If you consider that Jesus was thirty when he began His ministry, and that He probably began working with His dad learning from him at a young age, He was probably a pretty experienced carpenter. I bet He is a great carpenter. I just love that. No matter what problems you are facing, no matter how broken you may seem, or even how beyond repair you may feel, know that your God is a great carpenter who is more than able to fix anything in your life. If you will take your problem to the foot of the cross and leave it there, He will fix it. You don't have to worry about it, you don't have to tell Him how to fix it, and you certainly don't have to help Him fix it. Just bring it to Him and ask Him to fix it, He has promised that He will.

Thank You, Lord, that You were and are a great carpenter. Thank You that You are more than able to fix the problems I bring to You and are even eager to do so. Thank You for all the things You continue to fix in my life.

Day 16

> If anyone is thirsty, let him come to me and drink. Whoever believes in me, as the Scripture has said, streams of living water will flow from within him.
>
> —John 7:37-38

Have you ever been really, really thirsty and then drank something really good and had your thirst quenched? It is a simple pleasure but so enjoyable to work hard, become very thirsty, and then have this thirst satisfied by a cold drink. I played basketball a lot growing up and then went on to play in college, and so I have spent hours and hours playing and practicing basketball in the gym or on an outside court somewhere. To this day, when I pass a drinking fountain, it often brings back memories of playing really hard and then running over to the drinking fountain to drink some really cold water. For me, it is a precious memory and a spiritual lesson. Maybe for you, it might not be a physical thirst for water so much as a thirst for something else. You may thirst for hope. You may have gone so far from thinking or believing anything good about yourself or your current situation that it feels like you are in the middle of a desert with no hope for a drink. Before I became saved and accepted Jesus as my savior, I was spiritually thirsty but did not even know how to satisfy this thirst. All I knew was there was a thirst in me that I was unable to satisfy by myself; I was miserable and even desperate to satisfy that thirst. Then I discovered Jesus. David talks about this in the psalms. "As the deer pants for streams of water, so my soul pants for you, O God" (Psalm 42:1). The Samaritan women at the well would have to come back each day and draw water from the well to try to quench her thirst, but it would never last. God offers us so much more. In one of the last verses in the Bible, the offer is repeated: "Whoever is thirsty, let him come; and whoever wishes, let him take the free gift of the water of life" (Revelation 22:17).

Jesus is so kind and so generous. He invites anyone who is thirsty to come to Him. He is able to do so much more than we can even ask for or imagine. Imagine being really thirsty and going from that state to being so satisfied that literally streams of living water are flowing from you! How

Edward W. Hellman, M.D.

great is our God! Do you want to have your thirst satisfied? Come to Jesus with your thirst!

Jesus, thank You. In this fallen world that sometimes seems like a desert, I am so very thirsty, and I come to You. Thank You that You are more than able to satisfy my thirst. You are the only one who can satisfy my thirst like this. Thank You, Jesus, for inviting me to come to You with this need. Thank You that You are living water.

Day 17

> I am the light of the world. Whoever follows me will never walk in darkness, but will have the light of life.
>
> —John 8:12

Have you ever felt like maybe you have lost your way? You may have come to a place in your life that does not seem very good, and you may not even know how you got there. Or maybe you are pretty sure how you got there but do not know how to get out. When you can't find the way out of a bad situation, things may seem spiritually dark and even hopeless. You may even feel that not only is your current situation bad, but you are on a path that is taking you to an even worse state. Darkness can be like that; it is difficult to find your way out, and in trying to get out, things could get even worse. Have you ever been in a room when the lights have gone out and you are not sure you can remember where all the furniture is? Have you ever tripped over a couch in the dark? Ouch! In this dark state, you also have to be careful whom you follow. People will come to you with all kinds of advice, but it may not be good or helpful; it may even make you worse. As Jesus said, "Can the blind lead the blind? Will they not both fall into a pit?" (Luke 6:39). Jesus also says, "The man who walks in the dark does not know where he is going. Put your trust in the light while you have it, so that you may become sons of light" (John 12:36). People lost in the dark do need to be careful where they go but also whom they trust and whom they listen to.

If you have lost your way, turn to Jesus. He has promised that whoever follows him will never walk in darkness. It is interesting to note that light was actually the very first thing God created in Genesis. Imagine having the light of life with you at all times. Darkness is simply a lack of light; it has no defense against light and must disappear when light arrives. No problem you face can stand against Jesus, no matter how big it may seem to you. Choose Jesus and be in the light! Be encouraged that no matter how dark and without hope your current situation might seem, Jesus has offered you His light. It does not matter where you are or whether or not you feel like you deserve His light at all. It is His gift to you, and He really does want you to have it.

Edward W. Hellman, M.D.

Thank You, Jesus, that You are the light of life and that You have offered to share that light with us. I want to follow You, Lord. Please help me to follow You, and thank You for sharing Your light with me. Thank You for helping me overcome the darkness that confronts me!

Day 18

> I am the Door; anyone who enters in through Me will be saved [will live].
> He will come in and he will go out [freely], and will find pasture. The thief comes only in order to steal and kill and destroy. I came that they may have *and* enjoy life, and have it in abundance [to the full, till it overflows].
>
> —John 10:9–10, AMP

There is what the Bible says about the type of life a Christian should live, and then there is the stereotype of Christian life portrayed by the world. The world portrays Christians as living a life of lack—lacking fun, joy, humor, health, wealth, compassion, happiness, and really just about anything positive. A stick in the mud would be more fun to hang out with than this version of a Christian. But what the Bible says about how a Christian should live is not consistent with that stereotype, and Jesus did not live like that. Jesus came to earth so we could have life, and have it to the full, even to the point that He gave up His life for us. Understand that if you are living in lack or even feel like something has been stolen from you, that is not God's plan for your life.

Read and meditate on John 10:9-10. I love the amplified version; internalize it by taking it into your heart. It is the devil who comes as a thief to steal and kill and destroy. God wants you to enjoy life and live in abundance. How do you get to an abundant pasture, protected from the thieves? Go to the pasture that has a gate guarded by the shepherd; pass through the gate into the pasture. Go to Jesus. He is the gate; He is the shepherd. "He tends His flock like a shepherd; He gathers the lambs in His arms and carries them close to His heart" (Isaiah 40:11).

Thank You, Jesus, that You are the gate and You are the shepherd. Thank You that You have plainly shown us how to be saved—to go through You. Thank You that You gave Your life so we could have life and have it to the full. Thank You, Jesus.

Day 19

> Peace I leave with you; my peace I give you. I do not give as the world gives. Do not let your hearts be troubled and do not be afraid.
>
> —John 14:27

Have you ever gotten something you thought was free, only to find out later it was not? I remember one time when I was growing up, I thought I had gotten something pretty cool almost for free. If I would send in one penny, I would be sent six records from a list I could select from. Sometime after I got them, I started getting records shipped to me every month, but these I had to pay for. Pretty soon I realized that those first records I had gotten for a penny had not really been free at all but had actually turned out to be quite expensive. The world will give you something like that, giving something but always with the anticipation of getting something back, often trying to manipulate you into getting something more from you than you were originally given. It makes the recipient feel kind of cynical and like they have been taken advantage of. Have you ever felt like that? It is not a real good feeling, especially when you need help for something. Being taken advantage of can make you want to close up, build a wall around yourself, and not let anyone else in.

Jesus does not give as the world gives. When the world gives, it ends up costing you. Jesus gives us peace, and not just any peace but His peace. Could there be anything better? The Bible describes it as a peace that transcends all understanding. If your problem is a fire and His peace is water, imagine a lit birthday candle coming up against a river of water. His perfect peace is more than enough to help you through whatever confronts you.

Thank You, Lord, that You do not give as the world gives. Thank You that Your gift is perfect peace and that it is more than enough for anything that confronts us. Thank You, Lord.

Day 20

> I no longer call you servants, because a servant does not know his master's business. Instead, I have called you friends, for everything I have learned from my Father I have made known to you.
> —John 15:15

What an absolute privilege and blessing to think we are friends of Jesus! It almost seems arrogant to say that you are a friend of Jesus, but because Jesus said it Himself, it must be true. Have you ever had a really good friend, someone you would like to help in time of trouble? You would never wish anything bad would happen to a good friend, but you would welcome the opportunity to help a friend in need. Jesus has said you are His friend. He wants to help you, and He has helped you. In the Bible, He said He had the right to lay down His life for us, and He chose to do it. What a great friend we have in Jesus to help us in our times of trouble; as Proverbs 18 says, "there is a friend that sticks closer than a brother."

I looked at this scripture another way too, from an employer's perspective. When you have an employee who is honest, works hard, and has been there for a while, that employee really does transition from an employee to a friend. An employee may show up for work and even do an adequate job, but a friend will take ownership of the job and usually do it with excellence. A boss wants friends working for and with him, not employees; Jesus wants friends working with Him and not employees! He wants to be your friend! Isn't that an amazing thought?

Thank You, Lord, that You have made known Your ways to us through Your holy scripture. Thank You for the privilege and blessing to be called Your friend. Lord, please show me how I can be a good friend to You. Thank You, Lord!

Day 21

> I saw the Lord always before me. Because He is at my right hand, I will not be shaken. Therefore my heart is glad and my tongue rejoices; my body also will live in hope, because you will not abandon me to the grave, nor will you let your Holy One see decay. You have made known to me the paths of life; you fill me with joy in your presence.
> —Acts 2:25-28

A tale commonly depicted on posters is known as "Footprints." It tells the story of a man who dies and goes to heaven. He stands with Jesus looking back at his life, which is depicted as footprints in the sand. During much of his life path, the man sees two sets of footprints, representing Jesus walking with the man throughout his life. But during times of hardship and trouble, the man notices there is just one set of footprints. The man questions Jesus about this, asking why God would abandon him during difficult hardships. Jesus replies that during these times of trouble, the single set of footprints represented Jesus carrying the man through his hardship. What the man had interpreted as abandonment was actually Jesus carrying the load.

The scripture above, from Acts 2, actually dates back to a quote from King David. During much of David's life, he was harassed and pursued. King Saul chased him and wanted to kill him, so David had to travel from place to place, living in caves and off the land. Even his own son at one point chased him out of town and pursued him. But the Bible says that David was a man after God's own heart. He never lost sight of the idea that God was always before him, and so, rather than being frightened or discouraged, he was literally filled with joy in God's presence, regardless of his current circumstances.

Thank You, Lord, that You will not abandon me to the grave, no matter how dismal my situation might seem. Thank You for the example of King David. I know that if I will just realize and even visualize that You are always before me (as You are), I too can be filled with joy in Your presence and never be shaken. Thank You for the holy scripture You have given us that offers to "make known the paths of life" to me. Thank You, Lord!

Day 22

> But now a righteousness from God, apart from the law, has been made known, to which the Law and the Prophets testify. This righteousness from God comes through faith in Jesus Christ to all who believe. There is no difference, for all have sinned and fall short of the glory of God, and are justified freely by His grace through the redemption that came by Christ Jesus.
> —Romans 3:21–24

If you are anything like me, there are times when you just don't feel very righteous—even most of the time (okay, all the time). When I read passages in the Old Testament where God speaks about treating us according to our own righteousness, I sometimes get kind of uneasy. If I were to stand in front of God alone with the "accuser of the brethren," as Satan is known, listening to him list all the things I have done wrong in my life, it would be pretty humiliating. Thanks be to God that Jesus has promised to be there with us and intercede on our behalf, and that He has already done it! Thanks be to God that in scripture, God has promised to separate us from our sins as far as "the east is from the west." Thanks be to God that our righteousness is now not based upon our works or following the law, but rather we are treated as righteous by simply believing in Jesus. The Bible says, "For it is by grace you have been saved, through faith—and this not from yourselves, it is the gift of God—not by works, so that no one can boast" (Ephesians 2:9). God's grace is what saves us! By definition, grace is not deserved; it is a gift. If it had to be somehow earned by doing some certain thing or living some certain way, it would not be grace. You are not worthy, but if it makes you feel any better, neither am I.

There are about 613 laws in the Old Testament, and no one other than Jesus was ever able to be without sin. With regard to man apart from God, the Bible says, "There is no one righteous, not even one." We are saved not by following the law, but through our faith in Jesus.

Edward W. Hellman, M.D.

Thank You, Lord, for the New Covenant. Thank You that we are judged not by our inability to follow the law, but through our faith in you. The Bible says, "For the wages of sin is death, but the gift of God is eternal life in Christ Jesus our Lord" (Romans 6:23). What we are "earning" with our works is death. Thank You, Lord, for Your gift and that we are judged to be righteous simply by our faith in You and not by our works. Thank You, Lord! We love You and have faith in You. Please show us how to strengthen our faith. Thank You, Lord!

Day 23

> The God who gives life to the dead and calls things that are not as though they were.
>
> —Romans 4:17

The picture that has been drawn for you about your current situation may seem pretty well defined. There may have been a trail of doctors, and then family, and then friends who have all said almost exactly the same thing about your condition and your prognosis. What you have been told, and what you have been led to believe, and even what you may actually believe about what is going on inside you may seem very bleak. You may have been shown lab tests, X-rays, biopsy results, and expert opinions to convince you there is no hope. You may have been told you have two months to live, or that you would have to live in chronic pain, or that your surgery has failed. The things you have been told and believed and taken into your inner being may have led you to be discouraged, even clinically depressed. Take heart in knowing that even the things people will tell you are impossible, God can make happen. Doctors may say the cancerous growths you have in your body cannot be cured by chemotherapy or surgery, and that may be the case—but God can remove them from your body. God "gives life to the dead and calls things that are not as though they are." God is the final expert. The Bible says no one can shut a door God has opened, or open a door He has shut. Don't let anyone take away your joy or your faith in Jesus, whether they seem to have good intentions or not. It is God who is the final authority. He is the ultimate source of all healing power, not your doctor. God can use a doctor to heal you, but don't let your doctor discourage you or take away your faith. Talk to God and ask Him for help. Said another way, "We live by faith and not by sight" (2 Corinthians 5:7). Do not let what you see and think you know in the physical world detract from your faith in God.

Edward W. Hellman, M.D.

Thank You, God, that You do give life to the dead and that You gave me life when I was dead; thank You that the things we think we know and see in the physical world, You can completely take away, calling things that are not as though they were. Thank You that You do these things, not as some kind of cheap magic trick but rather out of Your love for us and Your concern for our well-being. Thank You, Lord!

Day 24

> And hope does not disappoint us, because God has poured out His love into our hearts by the Holy Spirit, whom He has given us.
>
> —Romans 5:5

Hope is only as strong as the object upon which you are basing it on. For example, you can have all the hope in the world that you will win the lottery tomorrow, but that still may not be the case. As we get more and more accustomed to placing our hope on things, rather than God, we also get used to having our hope disappointed. When we have a pattern of having our hope regularly disappointed, we can become discouraged and hopeless.

Isn't it great to know we have someone in Jesus whom we can hope in, and that hope in Him will never fail us, never disappoint us? You can listen to your friend's advice, or that of your family or even your physician, but put your hope in the Lord, and you will never be disappointed. As scripture says, "Delight yourself in the Lord and He will give you the desires of your heart" (Psalm 37:4). "Those who hope in the Lord will renew their strength. They will soar on wings like eagles; they will run and not grow weary, they will walk and not be faint" (Isaiah 40:31).

Thank You, Lord, that You have provided us with the one object we can have hope in that will never fail us, and that is You. Thank You that we do not have to search far and wide for this, as You have given us the Holy Spirit to dwell within us. Thank You, Lord, that in You we never have to spend another moment in our lives being hopeless or discouraged, no matter what the situation is. If we focus on hoping in You, I believe we will never be disappointed. Thank You, Lord!

Day 25

> Therefore, there is now no condemnation for those who are in Christ Jesus, because through Christ Jesus the law of the Spirit of life set me free from the law of sin and death.
> —Romans 8:1-2

If there is something you have come to believe about yourself that has caused you to feel condemned or even ashamed, know that this is not from the Lord. Sin is not the problem; the price for sin was paid long ago when Jesus went to the cross. God has said He separates us from our transgression "as far as the east is from the west." Don't misunderstand me; the Holy Spirit can show a person that behavior is sinful, and this can lead to a repentant heart. A repentant heart that changes its ways to follow God in truth is a good thing, but it was the act of turning away from Jesus, not sin, that was the problem.

I would encourage you to know that there is no condemnation for you if you are in Christ Jesus. If you find yourself felling guilty or even condemned, you need to change the way you think and focus more on Jesus and the tremendous mercy He has extended to you each day. The devil is known as the accuser of the brethren, but we have an advocate in court in Jesus, who has fulfilled any penalty you should have been sentenced to. His father is the judge. In Jesus, we have been set free from the law of sin and death.

Thank You, Lord, that in You we have no condemnation, and in You, we have been set free from the law of sin and death. As You say in Your scripture, "For the wages of sin is death, but the gift of God is eternal life in Christ Jesus, our Lord." Thank You that we were not left to get what we deserved through our sin but rather have received the gift of eternal life in Christ Jesus. Thank You, Lord!

Day 26

> For you did not receive a spirit that makes you a slave again to fear, but you received the Spirit of sonship. And by Him we cry, "Abba, Father." The Spirit Himself testifies with our spirit that we are God's children. Now, if we are God's children, then we are heirs—heirs of God and co-heirs with Christ, if indeed we share in His sufferings that we may also share in His glory. I consider that our present sufferings are not worth comparing with the glory that will be revealed in us.
> —Romans 8:15-18

What an amazing and humbling thought. Take a moment and really consider how great and awesome God must be. Really think about a power that could form the heavens and the earth, the stars in the sky, that could know each of the individual billions of people on the earth so well that He even knows the number of hairs on their heads, a power that knows and understands things so well, including the future, that even before a sparrow falls to the ground, He knows about it. And yet He has given us the right to call Him Dad and be essentially lifted up to Him as coheirs with His one and only son, Jesus. What a great, loving, and so generous God we have!

If you are going through something hard, you may feel like you do not have the resources you need to even survive, much less thrive. It can make you sometimes feel like you must not be very important to God. Understand this is a lie. You are incredibly important to God. You are a child of God! You are a coheir with Jesus! Jesus Christ is currently sitting in glory at the right hand of God the Father in heaven, and we are coheirs to that. That is our destiny! How awesome is that? There will be a time in your life when you will be living in such glory that you will look back at the sufferings you may be going through and feel they are not even worth thinking about!

Thank You, God! Thank You that in Your incredible might and power, You still thought enough of us to be so incredibly generous. Thank You that You have given us the right to call You Dad, that we have been recognized and accepted by You as Your children, even to the point that You have made us coheirs with Jesus. Thank You for the incredible glory You have planned for us. Thank You, Lord!

Day 27

> Who shall separate us from the love of Christ? Shall trouble or hardship or persecution or famine or nakedness or danger or sword? As it is written: "For your sake we face death all day long; we are considered as sheep to be slaughtered." No, in all these things we are more than conquerors through Him who loved us.
> —Romans 8:36-37

Consider for a moment what it means to say that you are "more than a conqueror." To me, being promised to be a conqueror would seem like it would be more than enough. A conqueror comes up against some type of conflict or battle and wins, every time. A winning football team conquers the opponent and wins the game. David conquered Goliath when he slew him, and this led to the army of Israel conquering the Philistines, routing them in battle. What could be better than that? What does it mean to be more than a conqueror?

I submit to you that the key to understanding what it means to be more than a conqueror is simply to understand the incredible grace of Jesus. A conqueror, almost by definition, would have to be engaged in some type of struggle or conflict that he would then have to win. We are more than conquerors through Jesus because the battle we may feel is out there has already been won by Him. If we had to "win" or "conquer" our salvation, it would not be grace; it would be by works. The Bible clearly says we are saved by grace and not by works; it is a gift of God and not from ourselves, so we may not boast. The Bible even says we are to accept it as a child receives a gift.

Thank You, Lord, that You have promised us that we are more than conquerors. We have come to our struggles, thinking we would have to do something pretty big, in and of ourselves, to overcome them. Yet You have already overcome and gained victory over anything that confronts us. Thank You that in You, we have already won. We have shown up to what we thought was going to be a battle, only to realize You have already won it for us. Thank You that You conquered sin and death on the cross so that we could live in victory here on earth as more than a conqueror. Thank You, Lord!

Day 28

> That if you confess with your mouth, "Jesus is Lord" and believe in your heart that God raised him from the dead, you will be saved ... As the scripture says, "Anyone who trusts in Him will never be put to shame." For there is no difference between Jew and Gentile—the same Lord is Lord of all and richly blesses all who call on Him, for, "Everyone who calls on the name of the Lord will be saved."
>
> —Romans 10:9-13

Are you in? On the surface, it would certainly seem like it would have to be a pretty exclusive club. If it were a party, you would expect security at the entrance carefully checking a guest list and just letting the "best" people in. If it were a job opening, you would expect hundreds of applications to be carefully scrutinized so only the very top candidates would be brought in for an interview. Think about it. Membership in this club is equivalent to being richly blessed by God. Is there anything that could be better than that? The God who could open the very gates of heaven and pour out every possible physical and spiritual blessing has offered to richly bless anyone in this "club." Not only that but He has established and shared with us the requirements for joining. The amazing thing about that is this: the verse says that "everyone who calls on the name of the Lord will be saved," and that He "richly blesses all who call on Him." Wow!

Notice there are no other requirements. It says nothing about our past accomplishments or lack of them, nothing about your wealth or what you do, nothing about your family or the side of town you are from. Anyone who wants to be saved can be, simply by calling on His name. It also does not say anything about time. As long as you have a single breath in your body to call on His name, you can do so and be saved. There is one fact that the Bible says is true about all people; at some point, everyone will kneel down and confess that Jesus is Lord. The question is really if this will happen while you are alive, and so be saved, or it will occur as a realization after you die, and so be condemned. There is no other requirement by

Edward W. Hellman, M.D.

which we must be saved. Simply recognize and accept the incredible gift Jesus has offered us!

Thank You, Lord, for the incredible gift of salvation You have offered to us. Thank You that You have offered it to me and anyone who calls on Your name, regardless of how unworthy we are. Thank You that You are so generous and yet also so merciful and forgiving. Thank You, Lord!

Day 29

> No eye has seen, no ear has heard, no mind has conceived what God has prepared for those who love Him.
> —1 Corinthians 2:9

We can see the works of God all around us. I just love to look at the beauty of nature, which I think in so many ways declares the very glory of God. It is just so humbling to think of all the things God already has done for us. As scripture says, "When I consider your heavens, the work of your fingers, the moon and the stars, which you have set in place, what is man that you care for him?" (Psalm 8:3). Think about some of the awesome things you can see in nature all around you: a beautiful sunset, a flowing waterfall, the multitude of stars in the sky, the vastness of the ocean, a magnificent range of mountains. As scripture says in another psalm, "The heavens declare the glory of God; the skies proclaim the work of His hands. Day after day they pour forth speech; night after night they display knowledge" (Psalm 19:1–2). Think about some of the most awesome things you have seen in nature, whether in person, on a nature show, or perhaps in a picture. So much in nature is beautiful, even miraculous, but we can still at least conceive of it. Yet, according to scripture, our minds cannot even conceive how wonderful heaven will be. When you are struggling with some hardship, think about God preparing an incredible welcome for you. When faced with a stressful situation, some people will resort to thinking about a happy place where they can think about something pleasant. They may think about a recent trip to the beach or an upcoming vacation and imagine they are already there. Think about your favorite place, and then think about why you enjoy it. Where you are going when you leave this earth will be so many magnitudes better than that. How is that for encouraging? You are going to a place so awesome you cannot even conceive it! How could you not love someone who is being so generous to you? Thank You, Lord!

Thank You, Lord, that You have already given us so much beauty here on earth. I am so excited about the things You have created for us in heaven, so great that we cannot even conceive them. Thank You, Lord. I love You, Lord.

Day 30

> For our light and momentary troubles are achieving for us an eternal glory that far outweighs them all. So we fix our eyes not on what is seen, but what is unseen. For what is seen is temporary, but what is unseen is eternal.
> —2 Corinthians 4:17-18

I initially hesitated to put this scripture in the book because, on the very surface, it just did not seem very encouraging. How can you tell someone who has been just told they have metastatic cancer that their troubles are "light and momentary"? Or it might not be cancer, it might be chronic pain that never leaves, depression that is so severe it is hard to even get out of bed and get dressed, or maybe they have been diagnosed with a terminal neurologic condition that is slowly paralyzing them. But consider how we really rate the severity of a hardship we are going through. We can only do this by comparing it to something else. So think about the worst thing you ever have gone through and trust in God. Be encouraged in knowing God has things planned for your future with Him that are so amazing He will make your current hardship seem light and momentary. I can give you an earthly example in my field. Spinal surgery can be tedious; sometimes we might spend six or eight hours repairing someone's spinal column and freeing their nerves from compression. And yet when we see the patient freed from the bondage of suffering and pain, the result makes it all worth the effort. And if your hardship is particularly severe, remember that God is going to take you to a place of eternal glory; that is His promise. And, as scripture says, all His promises are "yes and amen" through Jesus. What is the heritage that God has promised for those who follow Him? "No weapon forged against you will prevail, and you will refute every tongue that accuses you. This is the heritage of the servants of the Lord, and this is their vindication from me" (Isaiah 54:17).

Thank You, Lord, that You are taking us to a place of eternal glory that so outweighs what we are going through right now that it will make our current hardship seem light and momentary, even if it might seem very hard to go through right now. Help me to appreciate all the great things You have in store for me, and help me overcome the current hardship I am going through. Thank You, Lord!

Day 31

> Therefore, if anyone is in Christ, he is a new creation; the old has gone, and the new has come!
> —2 Corinthians 5:17

In some ways, you could consider life as a race. The Bible talks about running the race of life in such a manner that we will "get the prize." Can you imagine running a race trying to carry with you a full set of luggage? It would be hard to run, much less to win, and yet we do each want to win our race. For whatever reason, there is no question that life can throw some hard things at us: sickness, injury, job loss, divorce, abandonment, depression, just to name a few. It seems like instead of running a straight course, our paths get filled with the obstacles and the hardships of life. And in coming through those obstacles, the scars and baggage that can begin to accumulate can further drag us down.

Wouldn't it be nice to have a fresh start? Instead of getting up this day and feeling under some obligation to do the same things and follow the same patterns that have become your daily routine, what if you could just start your life completely over again? Not go back so much as start with a clean slate.

Jesus can do that for you. If you will surrender your life to Jesus, He will make everything new. Literally, you will be a new creation. Jesus has offered to do that for you and wants to do that for you. Be encouraged that today you can become new.

"See, I am doing a new thing! Now it springs up, do you not perceive it? I am making a way in the desert and streams in the wasteland" (Isaiah 43:19).

Thank You, Lord, that in You we are new. Thank You that we are a new creation. Thank You, Lord, that in You we are freed from our old self and are new in You! Thank You, Lord!

Day 32

> Fear not, for I have redeemed you; I have summoned you by name; you are mine. When you pass through the waters, I will be with you; and when you pass through the rivers, they will not sweep over you. When you walk through the fire, you will not be burned, the flames will not set you ablaze. For I am the Lord, your God, the Holy One of Israel, your Savior.
> —Isaiah 43:1-3

How incredibly encouraging! To redeem something is to buy something owned by someone else. We were essentially slaves; the wage we were earning from our lives of sin was death. That was our fate if no one had cared enough to intervene. The "default," if you will, for mankind at that moment, if nothing else was done, was simply to die in our sin. When Jesus came, He did not come to condemn or judge the world but rather to offer a chance of redemption of our lives from sin through believing in Him. "For God so loved the world that He gave His one and only Son, that whoever believes in Him shall not perish but have eternal life. For God did not send His Son into the world to condemn the world, but to save the world through Him. Whoever believes in Him is not condemned, but whoever does not believe stands condemned already because he has not believed in the name of God's one and only Son" (John 3:16–17).

So, if you are a believer, be encouraged that you have been redeemed and are owned by God! He has summoned you by name. He will be with you. Notice He is not saying He will take you out of the fires and waters and other hardships you may have in your life, but He is promising He will be with you through them, and He will not let them harm you. That is His covenant promise.

Thank You, Lord, that You did care enough to redeem me from my sin and death. I may never fully appreciate what You went through to do that, but I am thankful for Your love and Your incredibly generous gift. Thank You that I am Yours, and You will always be with me, and You will not let harm come to me in the trials I will go through in my life. Thank You, Lord!

Day 33

> But He said to me, "My grace is sufficient for you, for my power is made perfect in weakness." Therefore, I will boast all the more gladly about my weaknesses, so that Christ's power may rest on me. That is why, for Christ's sake, I delight in weaknesses, in insults, in hardships, in persecutions, in difficulties. For when I am weak, then I am strong.
> —2 Corinthians 12:9–10

When situations get particularly hard, they may seem like they just may be too difficult to endure. You may question whether your mind and body are really up to the challenges that lie ahead. It may be the start of the chemotherapy regimen you are supposed to begin next week; it may be the anniversary of the death of a loved one; you may be facing another surgical procedure. You may have a feeling of complete inadequacy, and it may be stealing the small amount of hope you need so desperately.

Please understand you are trying to carry a load you were never meant to carry. God does not rely on your strength; neither should you. God loves the underdog, and His grace is more than sufficient for what faces you. If you feel totally incapable of achieving victory over what faces you, delight in the knowledge that your God is with you, and He will grant you the victory you need. David was a small boy who had no business going by himself to battle against a fully armored, nine-foot giant, but he didn't go alone. He went with the Lord God Almighty. When you are weak and poor in yourself, you still can be strong in God. Sometimes it seems like some of the most amazing miracles of healing today occur outside the United States, often in very poor countries. We in the United States sometimes put our hope and faith in modern medicine. People in poor countries with little available medical care know they have no hope other than God. They know and understand that it is God who heals, and they totally rely on that. Their faith is often rewarded dramatically by Him.

Healing Grace

Thank You, Lord, that in some of the enormous hardships we face, we do not have to fight them in our own strength. In Your grace and mercy is our power and salvation. Thank You that You are more than sufficient and that Your grace is made perfect in our weakness.

Day 34

> I lift up my eyes to the hills—where does my help come from? My help comes from the Lord, the Maker of heaven and earth. He will not let your foot slip—He who watches over you will not slumber; indeed, He who watches over Israel will not slumber nor sleep. The Lord watches over you—the Lord is your shade at your right hand; the sun will not harm you by day, nor the moon by night. The Lord will keep you from all harm—He will watch over your life; the Lord will watch over your coming and going both now and forevermore.
> —Psalm 121

When you are going through a hard time, wouldn't it be nice to have someone to help you? You may have placed your hope for help in someone, and they may have really disappointed you. Please know that there is someone who wants to help you in your time of need, and He is the Lord, the maker of heaven and earth! He is powerful and mighty, and, as the scripture says above, He never sleeps. Isn't it amazing to think that He is watching over your life? And that He loves you? He will not let your foot slip. He will be with you wherever you go.

"Have I not commanded you? Be strong and courageous. Do not be afraid; do not be discouraged, for the Lord your God will be with you wherever you go" (Joshua 1:10).

Thank You, Lord, that You are the maker of heaven and earth and are so powerful and mighty, and yet You continuously watch over my life and will not let my foot slip, and You have promised to do it forever. Thank You, Lord!

Day 35

> But blessed is the man who trusts the Lord, whose confidence is in Him. He will be like a tree planted by the water that sends out his roots by the stream. It does not fear when heat comes; its leaves are always green. It has no worries in a year of drought and never fails to bear fruit.
> —Jeremiah 17:7-8

If you consider that we serve a God of limitless resources, that He could speak a word from His mouth and rain down abundant physical and spiritual gifts upon you, could there ever really be anything better than to be blessed by the Lord? He made the stars in the sky and everything on the earth. Scripture says He owns the cattle on a thousand hills. When you are going through hard times, you may need every blessing you can get. Really, we all do, but some realize it more than others. What does it take to be blessed of the Lord? Do you have to be holy, wise, or sinless? Perfect, strong, wealthy, or have had a lifetime of good works? No, and it is not related to your past; it is very much in this very moment. Will you trust in the Lord enough to go to Him with your needs right now? Regardless of your past and what you may or may not have done, will you trust in Him? If the answer is yes, then you know what? No worries! You will be blessed! That is God's promise to you, plain and simple.

By the way, there are other places in the Bible that talk about virtues that will be blessed, one of which is in the beatitudes in Matthew 5, which talk about blessing the poor in spirit, those who mourn, the meek, those who hunger and thirst for righteousness, the merciful, the pure in heart, the peacemakers, people who are persecuted and insulted because of the name of Jesus—not exactly the same group of people a Fortune 500 company may be looking for. God can use you even if you don't feel worthy; none of us are. God blesses obedience and trust, not a long list of accomplishments or an impressive pedigree.

Edward W. Hellman, M.D.

Thank You, Lord, that You have offered us so much. Regardless of what we have done, how we feel or act, or the situation we are in, You have offered to bless us simply if we will trust in You. And Your blessings are amazing! I want to be like that tree planted by the stream that bears fruit even in a drought and has no worries or reasons to fear. Lord, I put my trust in You. Thank You, Lord!

Day 36

> He who began a good work in you will carry it on to completion until the day of Christ Jesus.
>
> —Philippians 1:6

Have you ever had a bad day? Maybe you have had a lot of them recently. If it is said that there are good days and bad days, it might have been quite a while since you have had a good day. It may have been so long since you have had a good day that you forgot what they even feel like. There may be times during those bad days when you may have wished your behavior and attitude were better as well. Scripture says, "This is the day the Lord has made, let us rejoice and be glad in it." Yet you may have days when you feel frustrated, angry, even weary or discouraged. You may have done or said things you now regret.

Thanks be to the God we serve that He is a God whose mercy is abundant. Scripture says God will separate us from our sin as far as "the east is from the west." Notice He did not say as far as the north is from the south. There is a northernmost part of the earth (North Pole) and southernmost part (South Pole), so to separate our sins as far as the north is from the south is a great distance, but it is finite. On the other hand, if you travel east or west, you can just keep going; there is no end. To separate us from our sins as far as the east is from the west is infinite. I am thankful God is not done with me. Through this cycle of sin and seeking forgiveness and separating us from our sin, I am thankful for His patience and His mercy and that He is not finished with me but rather is doing a work within me. God is not done with you either. You may have messed up, but "He that began a good work in you will carry it on to completion until the day of Christ Jesus." He will never leave you or forsake you. He will refine and strengthen you. In your hardship, trust in Him and His love and His work inside you. Seek wisdom and guidance during all times of your life, particularly the hard times. Scripture says God is literally standing at your door and knocking at it, seeking to come in. Open your heart and let Jesus in, no matter what your situation is or what you might have just done. Don't wait until you feel like you are good enough. You never will be (nor will I).

Edward W. Hellman, M.D.

Thank You, Lord, for Your patience and Your mercy, that despite my sin You are working inside me and that You will not stop Your work until the "day of Christ Jesus." Thank You, Lord, and please continue Your work inside of me.

Day 37

> I have learned the secret of being content in any and every situation, whether well fed or hungry, whether living in plenty or in want. I can do everything through Him who gives me strength.
>
> —Philippians 4:12-13

If we made one list of things we thought we could do and compared it to a list of things we thought we could not do, it might seem a little lopsided. Sometimes it seems like everything we try seems to fail, and it just about gets to the point where we want to give up. You do what the doctor tells you, but you just seem to be getting worse; you are trying to perform well in your job, then you get laid off; you try doing something nice for someone, and they reject it. You know who could totally sympathize with you? Jesus! Jesus went around doing good and healing people, and He was persecuted. Jesus tried to help and spoke only the truth, but He was nailed to the cross.

But you know what? The tables have turned. Something happened after Jesus was nailed to the cross: He died, and then He rose again in victory. He ascended into heaven and is seated at the right hand of God. He has given eternal life to those who call on His name, He has given us the Holy Spirit to indwell in us, He has given us the Holy Scripture and its promises, and He has given us angels to serve us. Do you remember those lists? Jesus sees things differently than you may. The scripture says you can do *everything* through Him who gives you strength. Be content in God, be confident in the situation you are in, committing yourself to do all things through Jesus, the author and perfector of our faith. Remember Peter? When he got out of the boat and focused on Jesus, he could walk on water. It was only when he became distracted by the wind and the waves and took his eyes off Jesus that he began to sink. Focus on Jesus and then, as scripture says, "my God will meet all your needs according to His glorious riches in Christ Jesus" (Philippians 4:19). Not some needs—*all* your needs!

Thank You, God, that in You I can do all things. I am more than content to rest in Your mercy and grace. I am thankful for You, Lord. Let's do some great things together! Thank You, Lord.

Day 38

> For we do not have a high priest who is unable to sympathize with our weaknesses, but we have one who has been tempted in every way, just as we are—yet was without sin. Let us then approach the throne of grace with confidence, so that we may receive mercy and find grace to help us in our time of need.
> —Hebrews 4:15-16

There may be times when the things you go through are really, really hard—so hard you think no one can really understand you and your situation. People may even try to offer you advice, when they have absolutely no idea what you are going through or even seem to have the slightest clue about it. Support groups have developed for just about every physical ailment that exists as a way for people going through similar hardships to be able to encourage each other. Jesus is the ultimate support group. It is not just that He made you, that He loves you, that He knows you so well that He knows the number of hairs on your head, and that He watches your every move from heaven. He has actually been here and experienced what you have experienced. He knows and understands exactly what you are talking about. Are you in pain? Jesus was so badly beaten and tortured that scripture says He was not recognizable as a human. Are you in distress? Jesus was in such a state of distress that his body began to actually sweat blood, a medical condition known as hematohidrosis, which is usually associated with extreme distress. Are you not being treated fairly, or are people not being nice to you? Jesus was "despised and rejected" and, despite the fact He had no sin, was hung on a cross to die with common criminals. Jesus knows exactly what you are going through ... and even more so. What is Jesus's response? "I will declare your name to my brothers, in the presence of the congregation I will sing your praises." He loves you, He is there for you, and He is proud of you. He wants to help you, and most importantly, He does completely understand (and may be the only one who does!) exactly what you are going through.

Healing Grace

Thank You, Lord, that You did come down and live among us, and not as a ruler but as a servant who was mistreated, and in our worst moments in life, You know exactly what we go through. Thank You that You have invited us to come to You with confidence when we need help. Thank You for being there for us, especially when things are not going so well. Thank You for being willing and available to come down to earth from heaven and go through hard things. You are more than able to understand what we go through. Thank You for offering to help us and for helping us. Thank You, Lord.

Day 39

> You have not come to a mountain that can be touched and that is burning with fire; to darkness, gloom and storm; to a trumpet blast or to such a voice speaking words that those who heard it begged that no further word be spoken to them, because they could not bear what was commanded: "If even an animal touches the mountain, it must be stoned." The sight was so terrifying that Moses said, "I am trembling with fear."
>
> But you have come to Mount Zion, to the heavenly Jerusalem, the city of the living God. You have come to thousands upon thousands of angels in joyful assembly, to the church of the firstborn, whose names are written in heaven. You have come to God, the judge of all men, to the spirits of righteous men made perfect, to Jesus the mediator of a new covenant, and to the blood that speaks a better word than the blood of Abel ... Therefore, since we are receiving a kingdom that cannot be shaken, let us be thankful, and so worship God acceptably with reverence and awe, for our "God is a consuming fire."
>
> —Hebrews 12:18-29

When you are going through a time of hardship, your focus can understandably become quite narrow. There is a term, "losing the forest for the trees," meaning you can be standing so close to a tree that you may not appreciate the bigger forest. When you look too closely at a single piece of a five-hundred-piece puzzle, you may not appreciate what the entire puzzle will look like. It takes perspective, the ability to step back and realize the bigger picture, to sometimes guide you through your situation.

What is that big picture described in Hebrews 12? We are coming upon a joyous, massive party. And we are not, by any means, crashing that party; we are invited guests. Our names are written in heaven, and our kingdom will never be shaken, because it cannot be.

Mount Sinai is the mountain that represents the law. Moses went up it to receive the Ten Commandments. Anyone else who tried to approach God by setting foot on Mount Sinai would die. Mount Zion represents grace and the New Covenant. Jesus is the mediator of the New Covenant. Because of Him, we can confidently approach God without fear of death and join in the joyful assembly. Hallelujah!

Thank You, Lord, that You have written our names in heaven and that Your kingdom cannot be shaken. Thank You for the joyous assembly You have brought together and invited us to be a part of. Thank You, and we do worship and praise Your name!

Day 40

> I saw the Holy City, the new Jerusalem, coming down out of heaven from God, prepared as a bride beautifully dressed for her husband. And I heard a loud voice from the throne saying, "Now the dwelling of God is with men, and He will live with them. They will be His people, and God Himself will be with them and be their God. He will wipe every tear from their eyes. There will be no more death or mourning or crying or pain, for the old order of things has passed away."
>
> He who was seated on the throne said, "I am making everything new!"
>
> —Revelation 21:3-5

It seems that almost on a day-by-day basis, the level of rejection of God and His principles is reaching new heights throughout our society. As scripture says, "There will be terrible times in the last days. People will be lovers of themselves, lovers of money, boastful, proud, abusive, disobedient to their parents, ungrateful, unholy, without love, unforgiving, slanderous, without self-control, brutal, not lovers of the good, treacherous, rash, conceited, lovers of pleasure rather than lovers of God—having a form of godliness but denying its power" (2 Timothy 3:1–5). Does that look and sound familiar to anyone? But, as you see these things occurring all around you, can I tell you something else? When Jesus returns, He is not going to be returning to a beaten-up, broken, rundown bride; when He returns, true followers of Christ and the true church will be rising up, as the scripture says above, "prepared as a beautiful bride dressed for her husband."

So don't be distressed by what you see around you; don't be discouraged, fearful, or hopeless. Be joyful! Understand that the time is soon coming when God Himself will wipe every tear from our eyes and put an end to mourning, crying, pain, and death. That is your destiny. Share this good news with those who ask you about the hope you have despite the world falling apart around you. Be encouraged, become hopeful, and develop faith by focusing on Jesus. Love Jesus and others—and you have won the game of life! Nothing you are going through right now can even compare to that. Congratulations! Thank You, Lord!

Day 41

"For my thoughts are not your thoughts, neither are your ways my ways," declares the Lord. "As the heavens are higher than the earth, so are my ways higher than your ways and my thoughts than your thoughts. As the rain and snow come down from heaven, and does not return to it without watering the earth and making it bud and flourish, so that it yields seed for the sower and bread for the eater, so is my word that goes out from my mouth; it will not return empty, but will accomplish what I desire and achieve the purpose for which I sent it. You will go out in joy and be led forth in peace; the mountains and hills will burst into song before you, and all the trees of the field will clap their hands. Instead of the thorn bush will grow the pine tree, and instead of briers the myrtle will grow. This will be for the Lord's renown, for an everlasting sign, which will not be destroyed."

—Isaiah 55:8-13

I know what you may be thinking: *A forty-day devotional, and this is day forty-one!* My point is that the Bible is filled with incredible words of encouragement, amazing promises for you, and useful instruction. It is an everlasting, binding covenant God has made with you. I would encourage you not to stop at forty or even forty-one days. Get in there and discover all the Bible has to offer, every day for the rest of your life. As this scripture says, the word of God is sent out from God Himself and will accomplish His purposes. And what is stated as one of its purposes? It promises you will go out in joy and be led forth in peace, and this will be an everlasting sign for the Lord's renown! Think about it. God breathed, and the earth and everything in it were created. God breathed, and the holy scripture was created. The holy scripture will achieve the purpose for which it was meant. It is extremely powerful and is an incredible resource available to us. It is actually described and was used by Jesus as a literal weapon. You should be encouraged that you have this amazing resource available to you. You should familiarize yourself with the incredible promises scripture has for you and step forward and claim them for your life.

Thank You, Lord, that Your ways and Your thoughts are so much higher than mine. Thank You, Lord, that You have sent out Your word and that You have promised we will go forth in joy and be led in peace. Thank You, Lord. I trust in and stand on all the promises in scripture and all the plans You have for me. Thank You, Lord!

Part 2

BIBLICAL INSTRUCTIONS FOR THOSE GOING THROUGH HARDSHIP

INTRODUCTION

> For the word of the Lord is right and true; He is faithful in all He does. The Lord loves righteousness and justice; the earth is full of His unfailing love. By the word of the Lord were the heavens made, their starry host by the breath of His mouth. He gathers the waters of the sea into jars; He puts the deep into storehouses. Let all the earth fear the Lord; let all the people of the world revere Him. For He spoke, and it came to be; He commanded and it stood firm. The Lord foils the plans of the nations; He thwarts the purposes of the peoples. But the plans of the Lord stand firm forever, the purposes of His heart through all generations.
> —Psalm 33:4-11

In my opinion, right believing and right thinking are the two most important aspects of a person's life here on earth, determining if that person will live in victory or defeat. Do you believe in Jesus, His love, and know about all He has done for you? Do you believe in the precious and empowering promises He has given us in the holy scripture? Do you believe He took all your sin and all your sickness to the cross and paid the price for them, and that it is a finished work? Do you believe that His desire for you is to have health and to live in victory? If you do believe these things, what do you spend your day thinking about? Do you meditate on God's incredible love for you, His grace, faithfulness, and mercy? The Bible says, "Be joyful always; pray continually; give thanks in all circumstances, for this is God's will for you in Christ Jesus" (1 Thessalonians 5:16–18). Do you do that, or do your thoughts center on things that lead you to feel frustrated, angry, shameful, or afraid? Is your thought life helping you to bear good fruit and be a source of encouragement to others today and build your habits and character for tomorrow? The Bible talks about the heart being the place from which our beliefs and thoughts stem. Proverbs 4:23 sums it up like this: "Above all else, guard your heart, for everything you do flows from it." Perhaps it is stated even more strongly in the New Living Translation, "Guard your heart above all else, for it determines the course of your life."

Edward W. Hellman, M.D.

A minister named Francis Chan wrote a children's book called *The Big Red Tractor*. On the surface, the story is quite enjoyable, but it also has what I think is a quite profound point. There is a small village that raises all its food each year by planting a garden, and they use a tractor to help. The problem is they don't know how to operate the tractor. Basically, all the people of the town work together to push the tractor through the field, and with a tremendous amount of effort, they just barely raise enough food for the town to survive on each year. One day they find the owner's manual for the tractor, but they are initially quite skeptical about all the things the manual states the tractor can do. One farmer, however, reads the manual and gets the tractor running and working as it should, and then shows the townspeople all it can do. The people are amazed. The town goes from living in poverty with just enough food to survive to living in tremendous prosperity, able to share their crops and their newly found lessons with all the people around them. The analogy, of course, is with the way we live our lives as Christians and how we use and believe the Bible, the "owner's manual" for our lives here on earth.

There are Christians who believe, as the villagers above did, that we have to go through life using our own efforts to barely subsist, hoping things will be better for us once we get to heaven. And there are Christians who are, as the villagers were, skeptical. They do not believe that the God with all the attributes described in the Bible really exists. And if He does exist, these people doubt that He really wants to help them. What I can say is that I believe what is in the Bible, and I don't believe the Bible says we have to live in anything but complete and total victory right here and right now. The Bible says we are more than conquerors, that we can do anything through Christ who gives us strength, that He who is in us is greater than he who is in this world, and that we can even do the miraculous.

The first section of this book was a devotional, sharing scriptures of encouragement for those going through some form of hardship. This section discusses biblical instructions for those going through hardships to overcome them and live in total victory. God has entered into a very sacred and binding covenant relationship with us, the specific nature of which is described in great detail in the Bible. In this covenant relationship with the all-powerful God who created the heavens and the earth, He absolutely has given us everything we need right here and now to live in complete and total victory. The Bible is literally an inheritance filled with glorious riches and tools and promises we can use to reign as victors here on earth.

I will say that on one level, it was hard for me to write this section—not because I think there is any lack of instruction in scripture for overcoming hardship, because I believe there are many, but because it just initially seemed hypocritical for me to write about it. The truth is I have had many struggles of my own, and those close to me can well attest to them. On the inside, I am so passionate about my spinal surgery practice and so intense about getting excellent results in surgery in every patient every time that I know I am sometimes hard to work with. I have thrown staff out of the operating room if I think that in any way they are lacking commitment or capability to contribute to an excellent spinal surgical result in my patient. Is it okay for a Christian football coach to run a Christian football program by recruiting for the outstanding players and then demanding the very best from them in building a championship team—and then refusing to tolerate anything less? Is a spinal surgical program any less important than that? I know there is a balance between excellence in performance and compassion for others, and that balance is found in Jesus. I share these biblical instructions with you from the perspective of a fellow laborer, a person who has experienced struggles, and also a person who, by the nature of what I do, has seen and treated many people going through pain and suffering. It was a "homework assignment," if you will, that I benefitted from tremendously, and it is my privilege to share it with you. My prayer is that you will benefit from the scriptural instructions that follow and that your life will be transformed by them.

> "The time is coming," declares the Lord, "when I will make a new covenant with the house of Israel and with the house of Judah. It will not be like the covenant I made with their forefathers when I took them by the hand and led them out of Egypt, because they broke my covenant, though I was a husband to them," declares the Lord. "I will put my law in their minds and write it on their hearts. I will be their God and they will be my people. No longer will a man teach his neighbor, or a man his brother saying, 'Know the Lord,' because they will all know me, from the least of them to the greatest," says the Lord. "For I will forgive their wickedness and will remember their sins no more." (Jeremiah 31:31–34)

Before we begin looking at these biblical instructions, I would like to take one more opportunity to emphasize one very important aspect of the Bible. In the legal terminology of the times, much of the Bible is a description of the covenants God has made with man. The Bible spells out in great detail the nature of the covenants and the consequences of various behaviors by the parties within the covenants. It is as real as the contract you sign when leasing an apartment or buying a home but much more binding. The New Covenant is exceptional for two reasons: first, it is strong and binding; and second, it is incredibly generous. The Bible is divided into the Old Covenant and the New Covenant. To understand how binding the covenant is requires some knowledge of the nature of the ancient blood covenants. When two people entered into a blood covenant, they would become as one. All their possessions, all their debts, all their strengths, and all their weaknesses would become shared. The covenant would bind the two people but also their families together for eternity. In the covenant ceremony, a cut would be made, their blood mixed together, and the scar that remained would forever be a sign of their covenant relationship. The two making the covenant would exchange their coats, signifying a sharing of everything they possess, and exchange their swords, signifying a sharing of their strengths. The covenant member would essentially have access to everything the covenant partner and his family possessed. So, for example, if you entered into a covenant with someone who had one million dollars, you could immediately have access to and could spend all that money once the covenant was established. If your covenant partner had a vast army, your partner would be bound to come over and assist whenever you were in need of help. One example of a covenant relationship in the Bible was between Jonathan and David, as described in 1 Samuel. When the two made a covenant, Jonathan took off his robe, his tunic, his sword, and his bow and gave them to David. The Bible says Jonathan loved David as himself and that they "became one in spirit." Jonathan risked his life to save David from his father, Saul, and even when Jonathan died, David honored the covenant by taking Jonathan's crippled son, Mephibosheth, and treating him like his very own son by having him sit at the table to dine with him each day.

Jesus came down as God and man. He came down and received the punishment for all of humanity. Jesus was and is without sin. The Bible says that those who believe in Jesus are "in Him," and then, because Jesus is in God the Father, the covenant is completed. The covenant, which is entirely spelled out in the Bible, is also incredibly generous. It is almost like those who are in Christ carry around a checkbook with access to an

Healing Grace

account with all of God's limitless resources. In Christ, God is now our covenant partner, and we have access to all that is His. In case you think this is an exaggeration, consider just two of the many scripture verses on the topic: "If you remain in me and my words remain in you, ask whatever you wish and it will be given you" (John 15:7); and, "You may ask me for anything in my name and I will do it" (John 14:14). This covenant is a new covenant, completely different from the Old Covenant. The Old Covenant spoke of the importance of following the law. The New Covenant frees us from the law entirely; it is entirely based upon the grace that follows a saving faith in Jesus. There are two basic principles in the New Covenant. The first is that, without Jesus, everyone in the world stands condemned to receive the wrath of God, which is the judgment we deserve from God for our sin; that is the "default." As the Bible says, "For God so loved the world that He gave His one and only Son, that whoever believes in Him shall not perish but have eternal life. For God did not send His Son to condemn the world, but to save the world through Him. Whoever believes in Him is not condemned, but whoever does not believe stands condemned already because he has not believed in the name of God's one and only Son" (John 3:16-18). The second basic principle is that those who have a saving faith in Jesus are "in Him," and that because Jesus did receive the punishment for our sin by being crucified on the cross, at that moment all our sins were forgiven, we became the righteousness of Christ, and we have entered into a blood covenant with God the Father through Christ. We have essentially died to ourselves and become a new creation "in Christ," not by our works but by the grace of God: "But now a righteousness from God, apart from the law, has been made known, to which the Law and the Prophets testify. The righteousness from God comes through faith in Jesus Christ to all who believe. There is no difference, for all have sinned and fallen short of the glory of God, and are justified freely by His grace through the redemption that came by Christ Jesus" (Romans 3:21-24). "God made Him who had no sin to be sin for us, so that in Him we might become the righteousness of God" (2 Corinthians 5:21).

The name of the devotional is purposely called *Healing Grace*. Sometimes when people look at a list of instructions, they can begin to adopt a work's mentality. Christianity is based in grace, not works. God loves you even if you do not love Him back. He is faithful even if you are unfaithful. The incredible nature of the grace and love and mercy of God is not dependent on you or any work that you perform, whether good or bad. So why even include a set of biblical instructions? The Bible represents a sacred covenant He has made with you. It is an incredible resource describing in detail the very nature of the incredible inheritance you have received from God. Part of the inheritance you have received is the ability to live in complete and total victory right now. I do think there are times that traditional religion does not always emphasize this. Many Christians believe you have to live your life being beaten up by the world but that things will be better once we get to heaven—but the Bible does not say that. You already have everything you need to live in complete victory right now. The price for this victory was paid long ago; it was given to you by God, it is described in great detail in the Holy Scriptures, and it is your birthright. It is based upon a covenant that was made between God and your forefathers, it is eternally binding, and it includes you. We have a loving, almighty, and generous God who loves you very much and wants you to live in complete victory right now over anything that confronts you. I am simply describing some of the many biblical resources that are available for people going through hardship to totally overcome that hardship. Imagine trying to put out the fire of a birthday candle and having a river of living water at your disposal!

This section is divided into twelve parts:

1) Choose your foundation wisely
2) Prepare the way
3) Rest
4) Nourish yourself
5) Claim your inheritance. Do you want to be well?
6) Choose life—win your battle
7) Act like a superhero—give life
8) Ask
9) Praise
10) Be Jesus strong!
11) Climb the ladder
12) Go forth in the Spirit

> The same Lord is Lord of all and richly blesses all who call on Him, for, "Everyone who calls on the name of the Lord will be saved." How, then, can they call on the one they have not

believed in? And how can they believe in the one of whom they have not heard? And how can they hear without someone preaching to them? And how can they preach unless they are sent? As it is written, "How beautiful are the feet of those who bring good news!" But not all the Israelites accepted the good news. For Isaiah says, "Lord, who has believed our message?" Consequently, faith comes through hearing the message, and the message is heard through the word of Christ. But I ask: Did they not hear? Of course they did: Their voice has gone out into all the earth, their words to the ends of the world.

—Romans 10:12-19

1) CHOOSE YOUR FOUNDATION WISELY

> Unless the Lord builds the house, its builders labor in vain. Unless the Lord watches over the city, the watchmen stand guard in vain.
> —Psalm 127:1

> Some trust in chariots and some in horses, but we trust in the name of the Lord our God. They are brought to their knees and fall, but we rise up and stand firm.
> —Psalm 20:7-8

> I am the vine, you are the branches. If a man remains in me and I in him, he will bear much fruit; apart from me you can do nothing … This is to my Father glory, that you bear much fruit, showing yourselves to be my disciples.
> —John 15:5-8

If you think about the list of architectural and engineering projects that have been completed throughout the course of history, it is pretty impressive. From the great pyramids in Egypt and the former temple in Jerusalem to modern feats like the Golden Gate Bridge and the skyscrapers that dot our landscape, even the technology that goes into building a modern-day roller coaster, God has given us an intelligence and resourcefulness that has been used over the years to produce some impressive building projects. There is one building project, however, that has probably garnered more input over hundreds of years from leading architects and engineers than any other, and the mistake that was made at the beginning of the work has never been able to be corrected, despite man's best attempts. The project involved the construction of a relatively small tower in Italy, which has gone on to become a tourist attraction and is infamously known as the "Leaning Tower" of Pisa. There is nothing wrong with the tower itself; it is well constructed and is made of strong marble and stone. The problem is with the foundation. It was built on sinking sands, so it is unstable and has listed over to the side. No amount of cleverness on the part of humans can fix it. They have tried a number of things to try to correct the error but all to no avail. The truth is there is only one solution—which is to tear the structure down and then rebuild it on a strong foundation. This can be costly, time-consuming, probably frustrating to the people involved, but if you want a strong building, you absolutely must begin with a strong foundation.

There is an analogy between building a structure and living your life, and it is mentioned several times in the Bible. Jesus Christ has been described as the cornerstone that has been rejected by many but that can be used to build a solid foundation for our lives. The Bible talks about a life built on an unstable foundation as being like building a house on sand. When storms arise, this house will collapse, while a house built on solid stone will survive. The Bible consistently tells us we will have storms in our lives and that the way to withstand and even overcome the storm is to stand on the strong foundation of Jesus. For those who consider themselves Christians, it is also important to realize that the Christian life is not like a lunch buffet, where a person gets to consider what parts of their life they want to rely on God and what parts they don't. Consider a building of four pillars. If three of the four pillars are set in solid rock and one is set in sand, the one pillar can collapse and take the rest of the house down with it. Commit to wholly and entirely building everything in your life on the rock of a strong foundation in Jesus. If you are suffering or enduring some medical condition, make it all about God. Take a step back from your situation and make sure that every aspect of your life is totally committed to God. Do not separate this part of your life from God, and don't give the doctor you may be seeing more of your faith than you offer to God. If we stand on the foundation of our God in everything we do, we will never be shaken; we will always be victorious.

Is there a contradiction between saying we have to choose whether or not we will follow Jesus and saying we live in grace? Did I not say earlier that God loves us even when we do nothing to deserve His love? God could have made things different. He could have made us like robots that were programmed to worship and follow Him and even were continuously "happy." But where is the love in that? The Bible says the very nature of God is love. Love ultimately involves freedom. We have been given the freedom to love God or to reject Him. We have been given the freedom and resources to live in victory but also the freedom to live in defeat. We have been given an incredible inheritance, but it will not be forced upon us.

There is an incredible relationship between the Passover of the Old Testament, the life of Jesus, and our responsibility in accepting the gift of Jesus. The first Passover occurred in early April while the nation of Israel was enslaved in Egypt. The Jewish families were instructed to kill a lamb without defect and sprinkle its blood around the doorframe of the household. The angel of death would then "pass over" the household but deliver the judgment of death to the firstborn on any family that had not marked its doorways with the lamb's blood. Notice it was not enough for the lamb to have died and shed its blood; the blood had to be placed over the door and on the sides of the door for the judgment to be withheld from that family. Every year, Jewish people celebrate the Passover. In Jesus's time, shepherds would raise and care for special lambs in the fields around Bethlehem to be used for the Passover each year. The lambs would then be brought in and carefully inspected by priests for three days prior to the Passover to ensure they were without defect. It was these Passover lambs that were being cared for in the fields around Bethlehem whose shepherds were visited by angels telling of the birth of Jesus; that is why many biblical scholars believe Jesus was born around late March or early April, near the time of the Passover, rather than on December 25. Jesus was called by John the Baptist the "Lamb of God who takes away the sins of the world." He entered Jerusalem three days before Passover and was scrutinized and "inspected." Jesus was crucified, and His blood was shed for our sins once and for all. Jesus said, "Forgive them, Father, for they know not what they do." And then, "It is finished;" and after Jesus died, there was never any more need to shed an animal's blood to atone for our sin. He was and is the perfect Lamb that completely and permanently took away our sin. But notice that, as in the first Passover, we have to accept His gift; we have to cover our lives with the blood of Jesus. Said another way in scripture, "I tell you the truth, unless you eat flesh of the Son of Man and drink His blood, you have no life in you. Whoever eats my flesh and drinks my blood has eternal life, and I will raise Him up at the last day" (John 6:53-54). Put another way, anyone who internalizes and accepts the gift of the blood of Jesus has eternal life; he has essentially entered into a blood covenant with God. Entering this blood covenant does not just involve the acceptance of the death of Jesus and His blood; it also means we die to ourselves with Him. Everything He has is ours, but everything we have is His. Of course it bears pointing out that there is simply no comparison in giving up our meager possessions for access to His tremendous spiritual and physical blessings.

There are numerous Biblical examples of the importance of standing on the foundation of God, particularly when you might not fully understand what is going on or why you are going through what you are. Here are a couple of my favorites. The Israelites had been miraculously delivered from the Egyptians and brought to the very edge of the Promised Land. From the time God had delivered them from their captors in Egypt, He had provided daily food for them. When they complained they did not have meat, He gave them meat. When they complained about the lack of water, He made water come out of a rock. He provided a cloud to shield them from the hot sun of the desert in the day and a fire to protect them from the harsh cold at night. He made it so their clothes and shoes did not wear out; the Bible even says there was no one feeble among them. Basically, He was continuously with them and continuously provided for them. Yet when the Israelites finally arrived at the Promised Land and sent twelve spies to enter it, the report came back that there were large people and fortified cities in the land, and there were two very different responses. One group of people, including Joshua and Caleb, stood on the foundational belief in the strength and faithfulness of God and His promises; the other group, including the ten other spies, became frightened and completely lost faith in God's ability to give them victory in the land. They did not stand in faith on the foundation of God. They chose, rather, to become fearful, which led to an actual visualization of defeat at the hands of their enemy. They had abandoned their foundation and lost the conquest before the battle had even begun. What happened? God sent them back into the desert until all the nonbelievers had perished.

In the New Testament, there was a man named Jairus who was a synagogue ruler and whose daughter was very sick. He came to Jesus and asked Jesus to come and heal her. But on the way, people came and told Jairus his daughter had died. What did Jesus say? "Don't be afraid, just believe" (Mark 5:36). At that moment, Jairus had to make a decision; he was either going to have to believe and have faith in what Jesus was instructing him, or he was going to have to believe what the people had seen in the physical world—that his daughter was dead (along with the implication that there was nothing Jesus could do about it). Jairus chose to stand with Jesus, even when the crowds at the house laughed at Jesus. In the end, Jairus was dramatically rewarded by his faith when his daughter was raised from the dead. When given a choice, when faced with an apparent tragedy, Jairus chose to stand on the one foundation from which he could never be shaken. He may have remembered the advice given in Proverbs 3:5-6, "Trust in the Lord with all your heart and lean not on your own understanding; in all your ways acknowledge Him, and He will make your paths straight." As 2 Corinthians 5:7 says, "We walk by faith and not by sight." Things we may see in the physical world should not change our faith in God or His promises.

One of the things the Bible recommends to all of us, then, and particularly those going through a physical hardship, is to set the foundation of our lives on the rock of Jesus Christ. He is worthy and more than capable to help you withstand anything that comes against you. At all times, place your faith in the God who will never fail you, and He will be the cornerstone for the foundation for you that can never be shaken. I end this section with a warning, a favorite picture, and a favorite verse. The warning is this: If you do set your foundation on Jesus as your solid rock, there is nothing better, but you may not get a lot of appreciation from the world. The Bible says that if you are a friend of the world, you are an enemy of God. An alcoholic who gives up drinking may lose his drinking buddies, an employee who is no longer willing to bend the rules may lose his job, and a preacher who decides to preach unapologetically from the gospel may offend and lose his congregation. The Bible says everyone who wants to live a godly life will be persecuted. If you want an example of persecution despite being in the center of God's will, look no further than Jesus. Many of His disciples left Him when they said His teaching was too hard to take. But understand that making the decision to stand with Jesus is so worth it!

> Return to your fortress, you *prisoners of hope*; even now I announce that I will restore twice as much to you. (Zachariah 9:12)

Edward W. Hellman, M.D.

They say a picture is worth a thousand words, and I just love this picture of a lighthouse known as La Jument, off the northwestern coast of France. The picture is pretty famous; it was taken by a great photographer named Jean Guichard. I e-mailed him, and he was kind and generous enough to let me use it in this devotional for a small fee. To me, the picture of this man on a lighthouse in France in the midst of a storm is the perfect visual image of having Jesus as your solid foundation. If that man was in the water by himself, he would be in extreme danger. But standing on the rock of Jesus, he is safe and can be at peace. The storms of life will come, but Jesus is our rock on which we can stand in any storm that confronts us.

My soul finds rest in God alone; my salvation comes from Him. He alone is my rock and my foundation; He is my fortress, I will never be shaken.

—Psalm 62:1-2

2) PREPARE THE WAY

We talked in the last section about the importance of having God be the foundation for everything in your life and how things that are not centered on God will ultimately collapse and fail, even if they are in the life of an otherwise devout believer. A person whose life is entirely set on the strong foundation of Jesus will never be shaken; I truly believe that with all my heart. If you have ever seen a house being built, however, you will notice that there is a step that occurs in the process before the foundation is laid, and that is that the soil the foundation will rest upon must be prepared. This may involve leveling out and grading the soil in the area around where the foundation is to be laid or removing stones and other debris from the soil itself.

There is a spiritual analogy to this principle. Before Jesus came to earth to begin His ministry, scripture predicted that a prophet would come down to "prepare the way." John the Baptist then came down and preached a baptism of repentance to prepare the people's hearts for Jesus and His message. The book of Mark records some of the first words Jesus said as He began His ministry being, "The time has come ... The Kingdom of God is near. Repent and believe the good news" (Mark 1:14-15). When Jesus sent the apostles out, two by two, "They went out and preached that people should repent" (Mark 6:12). I submit to you that repentance is a critical but also powerful force in the kingdom of God.

For people going through physical hardship, repentance is also a powerful force for healing. To me it is awesome to think about what the Bible says about it: "There is rejoicing in the presence of the angels of God over one sinner who repents" (Luke 15:10). If life was a boxing match, an unrepentant boxer would be knocked down by sin and never get up again. A repentant boxer could still get knocked down, but he would just keep getting up over and over again. You could never defeat him. As it says in the book of Proverbs, "for though a righteous man falls seven times, he rises again, but the wicked are brought down by calamity" (Proverbs 24:16). If sin were dirt, an unrepentant worker would work in the field but never take a shower and soon would become absolutely filthy. A repentant worker might still get dirty working, but each day he would shower and cleanse himself. What is the spiritual analogy? Unrepentant sin continues and then leads to a hardening of the heart. Think about it. If you do the same sin over and over, at some point it will probably not bother you so much anymore. Think about a conman who steals from the elderly. It might initially bother him, but as he does it over and over, he gets kind of used to it. The Bible says people like that soon get so that they "cannot hear with their ears or see with their eyes." A hard, unrepentant heart may totally miss out on all the great things God has for it. Jesus gives a parable about a farmer who sows seed in different types of soil. The seed represents the Word of God. The seed sown on the hard ground was never received. The Bible predicts that in the future, some people's hearts will become incredibly hard. In the final book of the Bible, Revelation, God repeatedly sends down horrible plagues to the earth, and some people still refuse to repent, leading to their ultimate destruction. A repentant heart, on the other hand, repeatedly turns to the Lord. God promises that when a person does that, He will heal them. Repentance is an incredibly powerful tool for a person to use for healing; lack of repentance may make healing unlikely.

The gift that has been given us to repent in grace is such a generous and critical part of walking in victory and in health that I would really like to take a moment to discuss it in detail further; I think it merits deeper understanding. There is a way to repent in grace, and it is a tremendous opportunity for us, but if you are like me, there may be times when you have sinned and attempted to repent under the law and not under grace. What is the difference? To repent under grace means to accept the gift God has given us at the cross. Jesus took the punishment for our sin and took up our infirmities upon Himself while hanging on the cross. When He cried out, "It is finished," every work that needed to be done to heal us from sickness and to pay for our past, present, and future sin was completed. Jesus became the sacrifice for our sins, giving us the opportunity to be in covenant relationship with God the Father through Him. By accepting the work Jesus did for us on the cross, we know that we are "in Christ." When we sin, we turn from Christ. Repentance in grace simply means to change our minds and turn back to Christ. The Greek word used for repentance in the New Testament is *metanoeó*, which does not mean to work harder; it actually means to change your mind. Repenting under the law is different from repenting under grace. When we repent under the law, we often will confess our sin, ask for forgiveness, and then make a resolve to do better in our own strength to "work harder" under the law and not sin again. What is the difference in repenting under the law and repenting in grace?

Healing Grace

Repenting in the law is all about you and what you should do or not do; repenting in grace is about changing your mind and following Jesus. It is about Jesus and His grace and what He did for you; it is not about you. The Bible says we are not saved by works but rather by grace, so that no one can boast. What else does the Bible say? In Hebrews 8:12, God talks about the New Covenant He has made with His people. He says, "For I will forgive their wickedness and will remember their sins no more." The Bible says, "Christ is the end of the law so that there may be righteousness for everyone who believes" (Romans 10:4). Repenting in grace is not at all about trying to "do better." It is all about Jesus and accepting what He has already done for you. The Bible says that *in Him* we are more than conquerors, we have been forgiven, our sins have been separated from us as far as the east is from the west.

Make careful notice that sin itself is not the problem. Long ago, Jesus paid the price for our sin once and for all, and so sin has absolutely no power over us at all. When Jesus cried out on the cross, "It is finished," He meant it. The price for sin has already been paid. So the ability to repent is absolutely not about works but rather all about grace. The Bible says, "The wages of sin is death, but the gift of God is eternal life in Christ Jesus, our Lord" (Romans 6:23). When the prodigal son left home, he turned his back on his father and his family and everything he had been raised to be, and he lived a life of sin. Did the prodigal son come back under his father's good will by earning it? No, he simply changed his mind and turned back to his father. His father had been looking out for him, and he ran to him and embraced him and returned his rights to him as his son. It was the ultimate expression of grace, not works. The problem is a rejection of Jesus based upon the notion that we do not need to be forgiven and we do not need Jesus, that somehow we can earn our salvation through our own works and righteousness by trying to follow the law. For a nonbeliever, a failure to ever repent from sin leads to death. Jesus said, "unless you repent, you too will all perish" (Luke 13:5). A believer who at one point did repent and follow Jesus but who now rarely repents may bear little fruit and miss out on the blessings and life of victory that God has intended.

As I mentioned, repenting under the law and trying to do better does not take into account all the work Jesus did for us on the cross. You do not have to pay a price for your sins; it has already been paid. As the Bible says, what sacrifice for sins could possibly be left or be done after that? Or, put another way, "But this Man, after He had offered one sacrifice for sins forever, sat down at the right hand of God" (Hebrews 10:12). Jesus already offered one sacrifice for sins forever! Jesus puts it this way: "I tell you the truth, anyone who will not receive the kingdom of God like a little child will never enter it" (Mark 10:15). When a child gets a gift, does he turn around and try to earn it, or does he accept it joyfully?

The second problem with trying to repent under the law is that we are then resubmitting ourselves to the law again—the very law Jesus died to save us from. Can you imagine saving someone from being run over by a bus, and then seeing the person you just saved throw himself under the bus again? The law is holy. It was made by God, and it sets a standard that then reveals to us our sinful nature, but the law is actually referred to in the Bible as the ministry of death. Jesus came to save us from the death that would come if we tried to follow it. Many thought they were following the law and so felt justified, but then Jesus pointed out that simply hating your brother was the moral equivalent to murder, and lusting after a woman the equivalent to adultery, both of which were punishable by death in the law. Do you remember the Pharisee and the tax collector praying before God? By most people's accounts, the Pharisee was much more righteous, but the Pharisee tried to justify himself to God by his works, while the tax collector begged for God's grace and mercy, and it was the tax collector who left justified by God.

There is a third problem with repenting under the law, and it involves how we see ourselves. What we believe about ourselves will affect our thoughts, our actions, and every part of our lives. Let me ask you this. Do you see yourself as a sinner or as someone who in Christ has been made righteous? It may seem trivial, but it's not. "For as he thinks in his heart, so is he." This is what the Bible says: "God made Him who had no sin to be sin for us, so that in Him you may have the righteousness of God" (2 Corinthians 5:21). "God will credit righteousness—for us who believe in Him who raised our Lord Jesus from the dead" (Romans 4:24). "We have been made holy through the sacrifice of the body of Jesus Christ once for all" (Hebrews 10:10). "For I will forgive their wickedness and will remember their sins no more" (Hebrews 8:12). "Their sins and lawless acts I will remember no more" (Hebrews 10:17). Even in the Old Testament, the Bible predicts the coming of the New Covenant between man and God. "'The time is coming,' declares the Lord, 'when I will make a new covenant with the house of Israel and with the house of Judah ... For I will forgive their wickedness and remember their sins no more" (Jeremiah 31:31-34).

Healing Grace

I have often heard it said that the Holy Spirit helps to convict us of our sin, but the Bible actually says that the Holy Spirit convicts us of our righteousness. Read the following: "It is for your good that I am going away. Unless I go away, the Counselor will not come to you, but if I go, I will send Him to you. When He comes, He will convict the world of guilt in regards to sin and righteousness and judgment; in regard to sin, because men do not believe in me; in regard to righteousness, because I am going to the Father, where you can see me no longer; and in regard to judgment, because the prince of this world now stands condemned" (John 16:7-11). In that verse, scripture is talking about convicting nonbelievers of their sin, condemning the devil in judgment, but convicting the believers of their *righteousness*. Why would the Holy Spirit do that? In the old days, when people would enter into a blood covenant with one another, they would cut themselves and mix their blood together. Often they cut their hands to seal the deal, and this is how the initial handshake began as a sign of a blood covenant. This would leave a scar that would forever be a sign of the covenant relationship. The Bible describes the Holy Spirit as being a "seal", reminding us of our blood covenant with God, in which we have a righteousness not of ourselves but in Christ by believing in Him. I believe it is important to see yourself as God sees you and as the Bible describes, one covered with the blood of Jesus. He does not remember your sin and has separated you from your sin as far as the east is from the west. In Christ, you are the righteousness of God, and because of Christ's work on the cross and in Him, you are holy. That is way better than going around believing you are a sinner, and I submit to you it will result in you totally overcoming sin through Jesus by being *in Him*.

Another glimpse of the difference of repenting under grace rather than under the law is seen in 1 John 1:9. "If we confess our sins, He is faithful and just and will forgive us our sins and purify us from all unrighteousness." On the surface, it seems like the scripture is saying we should confess our sins to God so He will forgive them. But notice the words *faithful and just*, instead of merciful. If God were merciful, He would forgive our sins. If He were faithful and just regarding our sins, we would be punished with death; the Bible says what we earn with sin is death. What God is being faithful and just about is that we are in Christ, and as such, God is being faithful and just to the blood covenant we have with God through Jesus. As members of the blood covenant with Jesus, we are in Christ; our sins have already been paid for and forgiven. God is being faithful and just to that, not to our sin. Not to over-belabor the point, but again, to be faithful and just to us if we are asking for forgiveness for sin would be to punish us; that is what justice is for sin. Nowhere in that verse is the term merciful used. To be faithful and just to our blood covenant with Jesus would be to treat us according to the idea that our sin has already been paid for by Jesus and we are in Him; He has already taken our punishment for our past, present, and future sin.

This idea that all of our past, present, and future sin has already been forgiven is so incredibly generous that it literally takes a "new mind" to really accept this idea. It is the ultimate in grace. Jesus compared His message of grace to new wine. New wine expands, as do new wineskins, but old wineskins will not expand. So if you pour new wine into a new wineskin, all is good; both expand. If you pour new wine into an old wineskin, as the wine expands, the old wineskin will burst. To accept grace, one must repent from the mind that thinks it can be saved by its own works and the law rather than the incredible grace of Jesus. Trying to keep the law and earn salvation by your works can be exhausting. What did Jesus say to those who had put themselves under the law and were trying to save themselves by doing good works? "Come to me, all you who are weary and burdened, and I will give you rest. Take my yoke upon you and learn from me, for I am gentle and humble in heart, and you will find rest for your souls. For my yoke is easy and my burden is light" (Matthew 11:28-30). What is a better way to repent? Make it all about Jesus. Change your mind to appreciate the grace, the mercy, the promises, and the love He has given you; accept it as a gift you were meant to have and have already been given. People who follow the law will say that followers of this "grace message" will be steeped in sin. But what does the Bible say about those whose focus on Jesus and His grace and what will happen then? "And we all, who with unveiled faces contemplate the Lord's glory, are being transformed into his image with ever-increasing glory, which comes from the Lord, who is the Spirit" (2 Corinthians 3:18). You talk about wanting to conquer sin; how about by being transformed into the likeness of Jesus!

If you want a quick Bible study about the importance of not resubmitting yourself to the law, read the book of Galatians. Circumcision was one of the most visible, outward signs of following the law. In the law, the Jewish people were commanded to bring their newborn males to be circumcised when they were eight days old. After the Galatians received the message of grace and the Holy Spirit, some Jewish people visited them and tried to compel them to be circumcised. The decision to be circumcised after receiving the message of grace is resubmitting yourself to the law; it is not all that different from someone who sins repenting by resolving to do better by following the law. I would encourage you to read the whole book of Galatians, but here are a few excerpts: "A man is not justified by observing the law, but by faith in Jesus Christ. So we, too, have put our faith in Christ Jesus that we may be justified by faith in Christ and not by observing the law, because by observing the law no one will be justified" (Galatians 2:16); "I have been crucified with Christ and I no longer live, but Christ lives in me. The life I live in the body, I live by faith in the Son of God, who loved me and gave Himself for me. I do not set aside the grace of God, for if righteousness could be gained through the law, Christ died for nothing" (Galatians 2:20); "You foolish Galatians! Who has bewitched you? Before your very eyes Jesus Christ was clearly portrayed as crucified. I would like to learn just one thing from you: Did you receive the Spirit by observing the law, or by believing what you heard? Are you so foolish? After beginning with the Spirit, are you now trying to attain your goal by human effort?" (Galatians 3:1-3); "But now that you know God—or rather are known by God—how is it that you are turning back to those weak and miserable principles? Do you wish to be enslaved by them all over again?" (Galatians 4:9). Pretty harsh, right? He does not rebuke them because they are sinning; basically, they had received the message of grace and then also tried to follow the law, essentially resubmitting themselves to the very law Jesus had freed them from. When we repent by trying to do a better job following the law, we are doing the same thing. The way to overcome sin is not to try to do a better job following the law but rather to be in Christ and to accept His gift of grace and mercy. Repentance in grace is an incredible tool for living in victory and having healing.

There were a couple of other thoughts that came to me when I studied the aspects of repentance more deeply. First, repentance in grace is a radical change from what we were before Jesus, not just a small modification of how we think. The Bible says it is not like sewing a new patch of cloth on an old piece of clothing, which would cause the clothing to tear. It is like changing into an entirely new wardrobe! The Bible says, "Therefore, if anyone is in Christ, he is a new creation, the old has gone and the new has come!" (2 Corinthians 5:17). There is the obvious part in that verse that the new has come, but it is important to acknowledge the other part—that the old has gone, and must go. I also believe true repentance is a continuous

Edward W. Hellman, M.D.

process that goes to a very deep level within you. I submit to you that there are things deep within you that are deeper than your very beliefs and very much affect how you feel, think, and behave. Think about it. Have you ever become angry, fearful, or upset? And then when you actually thought about it later, you realized you had become upset about something that was silly to be upset about—maybe something that in retrospect you knew in your heart was not true. Maybe you were fearful about something you should never have been afraid of (can a mouse really hurt you?). Maybe you were angry about something you should not have been (the person you became angry with was doing something out of love for you). What that really means is that, for that moment, you believed a deception and not the truth. The area I am describing within you is probably not in you by conscious decision. Some of it may have come down to you through the generations; other parts may have entered into you as you believed various falsehoods over the years. It may be irrational, but it can have a large impact on your life. Even people who are sitting in pews of churches and following Jesus can become fearful, angry, lustful, covetous, bitter, unforgiving, and even resentful by believing for a moment a deception. These things can spin out of control and have a large impact on how we live our lives. Even the apostles, after they had been with Jesus, still became terrified when their boat was in a storm—and Jesus was even in the boat with them!

Consider two people who have the same big business meeting scheduled for today. Both people regularly attend church, pray to Jesus, and are hard workers. One person regularly repents, which is to say he repeatedly turns to Jesus. In doing so, his faith has become quite strong, and he repeatedly builds his life on the cornerstone of Jesus in making the foundation of his life. He has developed a relationship with Jesus and believes in his heart in the promises that God has made to him. His faith has become quite strong. He wakes up and rejoices in the day knowing that God will never leave or forsake him, that God goes before him, and that in God he can do all things. He envisions and is excited about the upcoming success he will have at the meeting. The other man rarely repents, and so when he sins, he goes for extended periods of time out of relationship with Jesus. He has begun to heavily rely on himself and his abilities. He wakes up fearful and anxious about the day, not only because he has forgotten the promises and love God has for him, but also because he has begun to believe lies and deceptions that come up from his inner self. This has become a frequent problem for him, and after his meeting, he has an appointment with his primary care doctor to discuss his medical problems, which have grown to include an anxiety disorder, high blood pressure, coronary artery disease, and a peptic ulcer. He envisions himself failing and maybe even losing his job, even though the meeting has not even happened yet. By failing to repent and turn to Jesus, he has essentially created and turned to a false god, and his life is progressively spinning out of control.

It all goes back to a common analogy used in the Bible. Jesus is the perfect cornerstone on which we can build a strong foundation for our lives. Faith is the path that takes us deep inside to build on that foundation. Strong faith is the ability to trust and go to God even when we don't understand the reason for our tribulation. In the famous "armor of God" discussed in Ephesians 6, the advice is given to "take up the shield of faith, with which you can extinguish all the flaming arrows of the evil one." In other words, when the devil throws something at you in the form of a hardship, it is faith that will protect you from being diverted from standing on the rock of Jesus. Will you trust in God even when you are going through something difficult? But even if we have the incredible opportunity to have Christ as our cornerstone, we are not forced to build upon Him. Our soil can become hard and rocky. We can choose other stones on which to try to build our lives. When we fear God, meaning a reverent awe of God, that is a good thing, and the Bible says fear of the Lord is the beginning of wisdom. When we fear anything other than God, we are believing a deception and going to another rock in our soil and building on it; the same with anger, greed, lust, resentment, bitterness, and so many other negative emotions. They are all based upon the deception that there is anything better than God. Whereas faith brings us right to the perfect cornerstone of God within us, fear (lack of faith) brings us to another god. The Bible specifically says God does not give us a spirit of fear but one of power, love, and self-discipline (2 Timothy 1:7). Fear rejects the truths and the promises in the Bible that God has given us and follows a deception; really, it is the original deception given by Satan that we can be our own gods. The Bible says that Jesus is the Way, the Truth, and the Light. Fear and anger take you somewhere else altogether. What is the answer to this? Continuous, radical, and deep repentance! Turning to Jesus softens the soil of our hearts and removes the rocks and false gods. "God is love." Jesus's "perfect love drives out fear." When a mature Christian goes through something hard, he or she does not fear but turns to Jesus. I like this verse from a Christian song we sing in church often: "The presence of the living God satisfies the depths of my heart." In the very depths of our heart, Jesus is all that we need; we have nothing to fear and everything to live for. When we go off track, repentance back to Jesus can help us realize that.

In summary, the ability to repent is a gift of grace given to us by God, and I believe it is a very powerful force in healing. To repent literally means to change our mind to turn to Jesus, to accept His generous gift of grace and mercy. "Let us then approach the throne of grace with confidence, so that we may receive mercy and find grace to help us in our time of need" (Hebrews 4:16). Repent and be healed. It is your gift waiting for you!

3) REST

> Let the beloved of the Lord rest secure in Him, for He shields him all day long, and the one the Lord loves rests between His shoulders.
> —Deuteronomy 33:12

> In repentance and rest is your salvation, in quietness and trust is your strength.
> —Isaiah 30:15

In this portion of the book, I talk about biblical instructions I believe have significance to someone going through physical hardship. This list of biblical recommendations may come off as seeming like a list of to-dos, but I do not want to lose track of the miraculous grace and mercy of Jesus in this task. In other words, Christianity is not works-based. Scripture clearly says, "For it is by grace you are saved, through faith—and this not from yourselves, it is the gift of God—not by works so that no one can boast" (Ephesians 2:8–9). You cannot earn your salvation. It is a gift of God. God is faithful, even if you are not. God loves you, even if you do not love Him. God gained victory over sin and death long ago. By His stripes, we have already been healed. The work that had to be done was already done on the cross.

So, with that said, I want to consider some scriptural instructions for those going through physical hardship that clearly do not rely on active works: rest, be quiet, and trust. Each is very important to the life of someone going through adversity.

I believe rest is extremely important in the life and health of the believer. We are made in the image and likeness of God, and scripture says God Himself rested after He created the earth. He designed us so we require rest regularly to survive and function well. I will even submit to you that God actually intends us to continuously rest. Don't misunderstand me; I do not mean we should sleep all the time. What I do mean is to rest from the idea that we have to do certain works or behave in a certain way to earn salvation or to make God love us. We are to permanently rest in

Edward W. Hellman, M.D.

the presence of Jesus. Consider this verse, which uses the word *rest* as both a noun and a verb: "For anyone who enters God's rest also rests from his own work, just as God did from His" (Hebrews 4:10). "Now we who have believed enter that rest, just as God has said" (Hebrews 4:3). Jesus wants to give you rest, as He says, "Come to me all you who are weary and burdened, and I will give you rest. Take my yoke upon you and learn from me, for I am gentle and humble in heart, and you will find rest for your souls. For my yoke is easy and my burden is light" (Matthew 11:28-30). The rest Jesus describes in this verse has two characteristics. First, it is a gift Jesus gives to us. Second, it is learned in part from a daily relationship with Him. This type of rest is really a frame of mind, an attitude. It is like having the attitude of peace and calm you might have while you are on vacation but having it at all times, even when you are at work. A biblical example is found in Luke 8, in which Jesus instructs the apostles to get into a boat with Him. A severe storm occurs, so bad that it threatens to swamp and capsize the boat. What is Jesus doing? The Bible reports He is asleep! Notice, Jesus does not say He will take us out of the storms we may face in life. In fact, the disciples got into the boat because Jesus had instructed them to do so. But the trick, if you will, is to be able to have a spirit of rest in the midst of the storm. This comes primarily from faith in the power, love, and supremacy of Jesus. The presence of rest in a person's spirit is completely incompatible with stress, worry, anger, and fear. Find your rest in Jesus alone, regardless of your circumstances. As the Bible says, "Cast all your anxiety on Him because He cares for you" (1 Peter 5:7). Or, as the Bible says, "Let us fix our eyes on Jesus, the author and perfector of our faith, who for the joy set before Him endured the cross, scorning its shame, and sat down at the right hand of the throne of God" (Hebrews 12:2). We all know the story of Peter, who looked out of a boat in another storm and saw Jesus walking on the water. When he kept his eyes fixed on Jesus, he was able to do the miraculous and walk on the water. It is only when he took his eyes off Jesus that he became frightened by the wind and the waves and began to sink into the water. At that point, he lost his restful state. To a person seeking healing, I believe the Bible advises finding a restful state of mind in the presence of Jesus and never leaving it; bring it wherever you go, no matter what you are going through. Don't let anyone take your restful state away from you by their actions or words. You are in charge of your state of mind.

Having a quiet spirit is also very important to the health of a person going through hardship. Jesus had a very busy ministry. There were literally thousands of people following Him around, listening to His every word, bringing their sick and demon-possessed for healing. Things got so busy at one point that even His mother and brothers had difficulty getting near Him. And yet it is interesting to note that on several occasions, the Bible makes a point to tell of how Jesus would intentionally leave the crowd, go into a solitary place, and have some quiet time. Among so many important verses in the Bible telling of the miracles of Jesus and His teachings, why would the Bible make such an emphasis on mentioning this? I submit to you it is because having a quiet time and a quiet spirit is important to the life of every believer. Why is it so important to have this quietness in your spirit, especially for someone going through hardship? I believe God wants to communicate with you, but it may sometimes come in a very gentle voice. Obviously, if your maker is trying to communicate with you, I don't think it is a stretch of the imagination to say that what He has to say may be important. Consider the story of Elijah in 1 Kings 19. Elijah was incredibly discouraged and running for his life; he was afraid. God offered to meet with him on Mount Horeb, the mountain of God. Elijah was standing on the mountain, and a powerful wind came by, then an earthquake, then a fire, and the voice and presence of God was not in any of these things. Finally, the voice and presence of God did appear, but it appeared as a gentle whisper. God gave Elijah an encouraging word, but I submit to you that if Elijah had not had a quietness in his spirit at that time, he might have missed it. Can I give you an example in my life from nature? In my medical training, I lived for ten years right in the middle of downtown Chicago. For four years, I lived on the twenty-sixth floor of a high-rise building, and the view at night was nice. You could see the lights of the city and the skyscrapers; you could see the Chicago River as it ran into Lake Michigan. Now I live in the country, and the nights are even more beautiful. Why is this? Because you can see the stars. In the city, the lights from the buildings would drown out the view of the stars, but in the country where it is dark, the view of the stars at night is remarkable. I submit to you that our lives can become so busy and so loud we may be drowning out God's attempts to try to communicate with us and fully appreciate His glory. We may be missing out on God's desires to encourage or even bless us by our loud lives.

We need to have a quiet spirit and carry it throughout the day with us. I heard about a woman whom I believe has a quiet spirit. I don't know her personally, but she has published books and led retreats attended by thousands of women. She is also a mother and a wife and leads many women's ministries. I suspect she probably has a very busy life. The story I heard about her takes place at an airport where she was traveling to a conference. She saw a man with long, unkempt hair, and God told her to go over and comb his hair. Though she was initially reluctant, she ultimately obeyed and combed the man's hair. The man was so appreciative, and she found it was a great opportunity to minister to him. Yet if she had not been quiet in her spirit and heard God, she would have missed that opportunity to serve Him. The woman's name is Beth Moore, and she is followed by thousands, and yet I submit to you that despite her busy schedule, she carries with her a quiet spirit that listens out and is obedient to God's attempts to communicate with her.

Closely related to being quiet is the concept of being still. The Bible says, "Be still and know that I am God" (Psalm 46:10), and, "The Lord will fight for you; you need only to be still" (Exodus 14:14). Being still basically means not being so busy in your spirit that you are not in relationship with God and what He wants for you. You can be so busy doing what appears to be important that you can totally miss what God has planned for you. There are even people working very hard in ministry and churches and areas of service that on the surface are doing good, but if the spirit within them has stopped being in relationship with God because they are so busy, they may be missing out on God's blessings and plans for them. The famous example of this in the Bible is the story of Mary and Martha. Martha invited Jesus to stay with them. She becomes busy making preparations for serving Jesus and His companions, but she notices her sister Mary is sitting by the feet of Jesus and not helping at all. Martha complains to Jesus, and scripture says, "'Martha, Martha,' the Lord answered, 'you are worried and upset about many things, but few things are needed—or indeed only one. Mary has chosen what is better and it will not be taken away from her'" (Luke 10:41-42). It would be certainly understandable that you would want to make preparations if you invited Jesus and His disciples over to your home, but what the Bible says is that Mary became *distracted* by her work. When you are going through something hard, you might feel like you are very busy, maybe even running from one doctor to the next, or from one test to the next; don't let anyone take away your still spirit to be in relation continuously with God.

Those going through physical hardships need to make sure we have quiet time with the Lord. We must carry a quietness and stillness in our spirit with us throughout the day that allows us to communicate with God, be blessed and encouraged by Him, and be a blessing and encouragement to others.

For someone who professes faith in Jesus Christ as Lord and Savior of their lives, having trust is where the rubber meets the road. Faith and trust are intimately wound around each other; you simply cannot have one without the other. If you have faith in God, you will trust in Him. If you don't have faith in Him, it will be difficult to trust Him. Trust must come from the heart, and if you are having difficulty trusting God, you need to check your heart and probe the very depths of the matter. It is hardship and trials that will sometimes bring our very core beliefs to the surface. It may be that you have professed Jesus as the Lord of your life, but when it comes down to it, you have put more faith in your doctor or your retirement plan or your spouse than you do in God. When these things fail, a person who has put his or her trust in them will be devastated. A person who really puts their trust in God will never be shaken because God never fails. There may be things that occur to us that we don't understand, but trusting in God will always be the answer to anything that confronts us. As the Bible says, "Trust in the Lord with all your heart and lean not on your own understanding; in all your ways acknowledge Him, and He will make your paths straight" (Proverbs 3:5-6). For someone going through hardship, trust in God is invaluable. There are times you might not understand what is going on, but there is never a time when trust in God will not be the answer for those times. How can you get this trust if you are having difficulty getting it, particularly when it is so important? God has promised to help us. Remember trust must come from the heart, but God has promised to guard our very hearts in scripture: "Do not be anxious about anything, but in everything, by prayer and petition, with thanksgiving, present your request to God. And the peace of God, which transcends all understanding, will guard your hearts and minds in Christ Jesus" (Philippians 4:6-7).

The other part of trust is the ability to wait, or be patient, which basically means to trust in the timing of God. When God gave the Israelites the Promised Land, He did not give it to them all at once. He gave it to them over years and after many conquests. As He said in the holy scripture, He gave it to them "little by little." The perfect time to receive a blessing is when God wants to give it to you, not always when you want it. I trust in God's timing more than my judgment. In addition, waiting for a much-needed

Edward W. Hellman, M.D.

blessing develops perseverance, and "Perseverance must finish its work, so that you may be mature and complete, not lacking anything" (James 1:4).

So I would say to those going through hardship—trust in God. Lean not on our own understanding. If you are having trouble fully trusting God, pray to Him with a thankful heart. Ask Him for help, and He will guard your heart and mind, where faith and trust originate.

4) NOURISH YOURSELF

In the field of medicine, nourishment is extremely important to a person's health. Good nourishment strengthens a patient and empowers that person's body to fight physical illness and disease. Lack of nourishment is consistently associated with poorer outcomes in just about every physical condition a doctor will see. In the field of orthopedics, malnourishment is one of the highest risk factors for a poor outcome or complication from a surgical procedure. Almost 70 percent of a person's immune system is located in the gut, and so nourishing a person can also dramatically strengthen the immune system to fight disease. Doctors are becoming increasingly aware of the importance of proper nourishment to fight any physical hardship a patient may face.

The Bible itself is a critical part of our nourishment. Jesus Himself said, "It is written: Man does not live on bread alone, but on every word that comes from the mouth of God" (Matthew 4:4). He said this when He was under attack by Satan. I would like to take a moment to talk about the Bible itself and how remarkable it is, and then we will discuss its benefits as it relates to health and healing.

The Bible itself, our holy scripture, is an amazing resource to every Christian. There are some who believe it is simply a historical book that may be entertaining or may have some life lessons but is nothing more. Many consider the Bible to be antiquated, irrelevant to issues and problems we face in modern times. I believe with all my heart that the Bible is what it says it is. It is actually alive and is active. It is actually the very words of God, and it has the ability to literally transform us. If someone is going through difficult times of physical hardship, the Bible can heal him or her. The word "Bible" means book or scroll. The term "scripture" means sacred writings. "Gospel" literally means good news, but one of the things the Bible really represents is a covenant between God and man. The Bible says, "And you are heirs of the prophets and of the covenant God made with your fathers" (Acts 3:24). In these modern times, it may be difficult to fully appreciate the significance of a covenant relationship because we simply don't have anything like it. Two people and their families for generations to come were literally joined together. When David made a covenant relationship with Jonathan, for example, the Bible says they became "one in spirit" and "he loved him as himself." Jonathan took off his royal robe, sword, bow and belt and gave them to David; Jonathan even risked his own life to keep David from harm from Saul, his father. When Jonathan was killed in battle, David honored his covenant with him by searching out his crippled son, Mephiboseth, and restoring his family's wealth to him and having him eat at David's table. In terms of relationships, there was really nothing stronger then, nor is there anything stronger now, than a covenant relationship between two people. "I am as you are, my people as your people, my horses as your horses" (1 Kings 22:4). So when you think about the Bible as being an extremely powerful covenant relationship God made with your forefathers and with you, it should really change the way you look at it. In covenant relationship ceremonies, the blood of the two participants was shed and mixed together, signifying two becoming one. The Bible is filled with the promises He has given you as part of the binding covenant you are a part of. It is really incredible to fully try to appreciate what God has done for us, but it is all described in detail in the Bible. Being in right relationship with God and His Word is more than enough to live in complete and total victory right here and right now, because of His incredible grace and mercy He has extended to us. Here is just one example of the many covenant promises God has made with us:

> "So now I have sworn not to be angry with you, never to rebuke you again. Though the mountains be shaken and the hills be removed, yet my unfailing love for you will not be shaken nor my covenant of peace be removed," says the Lord who has compassion on you. "Afflicted city, lashed by storms and not comforted, I will rebuild you with stones of turquoise, your foundations with sapphires. I will make your battlements of rubies, your gates of sparkling jewels, and all your walls of precious stones. All your sons will be taught by the Lord, and great will be your children's peace. In righteousness you will be established: Tyranny will be far from you; you will have nothing to fear. Terror will be far removed; it will not come near you. If anyone does attack you, it will not be my doing; whoever attacks you will surrender to you. See, it is I who created the blacksmith who fans the coals into flame and forges a weapon fit for its work. And it is I who have created the destroyer to work havoc; no weapon forged against you will prevail, and you will refute every tongue that accuses you. This is the heritage of the servants of the Lord, and this is their vindication from me," declares the Lord. (Isaiah 54:9–17)

This is just one of the many promises God has made to you in His covenant with you.

Consider also, for a moment, some of the facts about the Bible so you can more fully appreciate how remarkable it is. The Bible itself has been persecuted, and many attempts have been made throughout history to completely eradicate it. It is still illegal in many countries throughout the world today, and yet it is the best-selling, most widely distributed book of all time. Year after year, it continues to be the best-selling book in the United States and throughout the world. Despite its persecution, there are currently approximately 128,000 Bibles sold or given away each day throughout the world! The Bible was written by over forty authors over a span of over fifteen hundred years. The authors included kings, peasants, fisherman, scholars, poets, statesman, and all walks of life on three continents, and yet the messages of the Bible are all in complete harmony with each other; there are no contradictions. As a historical book, the Bible has proven to be completely accurate, and there have never been any archaeological finds that have contradicted the Bible. There have been many examples where archaeologists have criticized the Bible and then later found out the historical facts were true as newly discovered sites proved the archaeologists wrong. The Bible even predicted the four major empires of the world—Babylonian, Mede-Persia, Greek, and Roman—and that the Roman empire would be broken into ten parts, which became the ten countries in Europe, all hundreds of years before these events occurred. As a scientific book, the Bible has revealed facts that were not appreciated until well after they were written, sometimes even hundreds of years later. For example, at the time much of the Bible was written, people widely held that the earth was flat and rested on something, and yet at that time the Bible said the earth was round and free floating; it was hundreds of years later that this was discovered to be true. The Bible says we are made up of such small particles that they cannot be seen, and yet it was hundreds of years before things like the atom were discovered. The Bible instructs people to wash in flowing water and to carefully dispose of their waste, and yet for years after, people would wash in stagnant water and not properly dispose of their waste, causing sickness and death. It was only years later that it was discovered that proper hygiene practices were a way to avoid sicknesses. The story of Noah gives a detailed description of the construction of the ark. To this day, the length-to-width dimensions given for the ark are still widely accepted as ideal proportions for seagoing vessels.

Edward W. Hellman, M.D.

More than a hundred scientific facts like this were not fully appreciated by the scientific community until well after they were written in the Bible. The Bible contains over three thousand prophecies that have been fulfilled, and over three thousand prophecies that have not yet been fulfilled. In the Old Testament, there are over three hundred prophecies talking about the coming of Jesus, despite the fact that the last book of the Old Testament was written more than four hundred years before Jesus was born. The Old Testament predicts when Jesus would be born, where He would be born, that He would be born of a virgin, that He would suffer and be beaten, that He would be betrayed, that He would be of the line of Judah, Jesse, and David, that He would be poor, that He would be crucified, that His body would be pierced, and that He would die for us, among many other prophecies. A mathematician has measured the odds of just some of these predictions happening by chance and equated them to the odds of picking one specific coin out of a pile of silver dollars covering the whole state of Texas to a depth of two feet—the chances are essentially one in ten to the seventeenth power! The apostles of Jesus were so convinced He was the Messiah that they themselves continued His ministry after His death and resurrection despite severe persecution, torture, and death. Historical records reveal that eleven of the twelve apostles were put to death for their beliefs. The lone exception to this was John; an attempt to poison and kill him was unsuccessful, and ultimately he was exiled to the island of Patmos. If the apostles were part of some scam to somehow make up the story of Jesus as Messiah, they went to extraordinary lengths to hide it. They were beaten, persecuted, and killed for what they clearly and passionately believed in.

The Bible is certainly more than a simple book. If you consider the content of the Bible to be true, it becomes even more amazing in what it says about itself, especially for someone going through a physical hardship such as chronic illness, cancer, imprisonment, pain, addiction, or even recovery from surgery. It is living and active; it is the very word of God. It has the capability to heal us, and it can be used as a weapon. It has promises for us that we can use, it encourages us and instructs us, it empowers us and protects us, and it can save us. It is really a remarkable resource for a Christian, and it is probably underused by many of us. But I do think the attitude with which you read the Bible is critical. Do you believe that scripture is the inerrant word of God, sent to guide, encourage, and empower you? If you don't believe this, then you may not get much out of it. The Bible itself talks about people who have ears but do not hear, and eyes but do not see, and much of the book describes people who have calloused hearts that are not really open to what God has to say. It should be noted that even Satan knows scripture and tried to use it to trick Jesus. But if you will read the Bible with the reverent awe that it was intended, and with an open heart, and then take it into your heart, being obedient and doing what it says, you will be amazed and transformed by what you experience by the reading and following of His Word. What good does it do to believe in a medicine or even food but then not take it into your body? Scripture is meant to be internalized. Jesus was constantly using scripture in His ministry as we should in ours; it was a part of His very being, as it should be in ours. Jesus is even described in the Bible as "the Word": "The Word became flesh and made His dwelling among us. We have seen His glory, the glory of the One and Only, who came from the Father full of grace and truth."

Here is a small sample of what scripture says about itself, particularly as it relates to health and healing:

> My son, pay attention to what I say; listen closely to my words. Do not let them out of your sight, keep them within your heart; for they are life to those who find them and health to a man's whole body.
> —Proverbs 4:20-22

> He sent forth his word and healed them; He rescued them from the grave.
> —Psalm 107:20

> All Scripture is God-breathed and is useful for teaching, rebuking, correcting, and training in righteousness, so that the man of God may be thoroughly equipped for every good work.
> —2 Timothy 3:16-17

> The Son is the radiance of God's glory and the exact representation of His being, sustaining all things by His powerful word.
> —Hebrews 1:3

Edward W. Hellman, M.D.

As the rain and snow come down from heaven, and do not return to it without watering the earth and making it bud and flourish, so that it yields seed for the sower and bread for the eater, so is my word that goes out from my mouth: It will not return to me empty, but will accomplish what I desire and achieve the purpose for which I sent it.
—Isaiah 55:10-11

For the word of God is living and active. Sharper than any double edged sword, it penetrates even to dividing soul and spirit, joints and marrow.
—Hebrews 4:12

Worship the Lord your God, and his blessing will be on your food and water. I will take away your sickness from among you.
—Exodus 23:25

O Lord my God, I called to you for help and you healed me.
—Psalm 30:2

If you listen carefully to the voice of the Lord your God and do what is right in His eyes, if you pay attention to His commands and keep all His decrees, I will not bring on you any of the diseases I brought on the Egyptians, for I am the Lord, who heals you.
—Exodus 15:26

Praise the Lord, O my soul, and forget not all his benefits—who forgives all your sins and heals all your diseases.
—Psalm 103:2-3

He sent forth His word and healed them: He rescued them from the grave.
—Psalm 107:20

Therefore, there is now no condemnation for those who are in Christ Jesus, because through Christ Jesus the law of the Spirit of life set me free from the law of sin and death.
—Romans 8:1-2

Take to heart all the words I have solemnly declared to you this day, so that you may command all your children to obey carefully all the words of this law. They are not just idle words for you—they are your life. By them you will live long in the land you are crossing the Jordan to possess.
—Deuteronomy 32:46-47

As for God, His way is perfect: the word of the Lord is flawless; He is a shield for all who take refuge in Him.
—2 Samuel 22:31

Your word is a lamp to my feet, and a light for my path.
—Psalm 119:105

But the man who looks intently into the perfect law that gives freedom, and continues to do this, not forgetting what he has heard, but doing it—he will be blessed in what he does.
—James 1:25

In the beginning was the Word, and the Word was with God, and the Word was God. He was with God in the beginning. Through him all things were made; without Him nothing was made that has been made. In Him was life, and that life was the light of men. The light shines in darkness, but the darkness has not understood it.
—John 1:1-5

The Word became flesh and made His dwelling among us. We have seen His glory, the glory of the One and Only, who came from the Father, full of grace and truth.
—John 1:14

Edward W. Hellman, M.D.

> Now brothers, I want to remind you of the gospel I preached to you, which you received and on which you have taken your stand. By this gospel you are saved, if you hold firmly to the word I preached to you.
> —1 Corinthians 15:1-2

> "But I will restore your health and heal your wounds," declares the Lord.
> —Jeremiah 30:17

> The law of the Lord is perfect, reviving the soul. The statutes of the Lord are trustworthy, making wise the simple. The precepts of the Lord are right, giving joy to the heart. The commands of the Lord are radiant, giving light to the eyes. The fear of the Lord is pure, enduring forever. The ordinances of the Lord are sure and all together righteous. They are more precious than gold, than much pure gold; they are sweeter than honey, than honey from the comb. By them is your servant warned; in keeping them is great reward.
> —Psalm 19:7-11

> My prayer is not that you take them out of the world but that you protect them from the evil one. They are not of the world, even as I am not of it. Sanctify them by the truth; your word is truth. As you sent me into the world, I have sent them into the world. For them I sanctify myself, that they too may be truly sanctified.
> —John 17:15-19

The holy scripture has many amazing resources for us, and among these is the ability to heal. We will talk more about some specific resources of the Bible for healing in future sections, but at this point, I would like to encourage you to read the Bible often. Read it, let it soak in to you, and take it into your heart, mind, and soul. Internalize it and meditate on it. You will find it is the best medicine ever created. It will transform your life and your health. Take it daily, and take it into your heart. Nourish yourself with it!

5) CLAIM YOUR INHERITANCE DO YOU WANT TO BE WELL?

> His divine power has given us everything we need for life and godliness through our knowledge of Him who called us by His own glory and goodness. Through these He has given us His very great and precious promises, so that through them you may participate in the divine nature and escape the corruption in the world caused by evil desires.
> —2 Peter 1:3–4

> And you are heirs of the prophets and the covenant God made with your fathers.
> —Acts 3:24

Do you want to be well? For someone going through a physical hardship, this question runs the risk of being offensive, because it suggests the person has intentionally chosen not to be well. Yet it is an extremely important, even critical question. Why do I believe it is such an important question? Because Jesus asked it, and it is recorded in scripture. In John 5, Jesus asked this question right before He healed a man who had been crippled for thirty-eight years. The amazing thing to me is that, before the man did get healed, he may not have even known who Jesus was, nor is there a record that he even asked Jesus to be healed. He may not have even appreciated that Jesus could heal him. When asked, "Do you want to be well?" the man responded by describing what he believed was an insurmountable problem. The man was lying at a pool named Bethesda. Bethesda was a pool where disabled people would come in the hope of being healed. It was felt that when the water became stirred, a person could bathe in the pool and be healed. But because the man was crippled and had no one to help him, he stated that every time the water was stirred, someone else would get in the water ahead of him. In his own way, I believe he was asking Jesus to help him, and Jesus did more than the man asked for or probably even imagined!

Edward W. Hellman, M.D.

To some degree, we were all once like the crippled man in Bethesda, badly needing Jesus to heal us. Before we were born, Jesus came and died for our sins, redeeming us from sin and death and offering us the chance of eternal life with Him in heaven. Salvation is ultimately about realizing we have a problem called sin that is insurmountable to us by ourselves; when we turn to Jesus for help, Jesus can and will do more than we could ever ask or imagine. The story of the crippled man at Bethesda is the story of the offering of salvation to us all. Praise be to God that He did save us from our wretched state! There may not be any condition that is worse, however, than not even to realize the wretched state you are in. There is a term that is used by the world to describe a man who has prospered and does not feel like he needs Jesus. He is called a "self-made man." But from a Christian perspective, this is equivalent to another term, "dead man walking," which describes a person in prison waiting for the outcome of their death sentence, the execution. The only thing that can save that man is a pardon. The only thing that can save us from death is the redemption of Jesus, and the sooner we realize that, the better. Just as many alcoholics may have to reach rock bottom before they will seek help, whatever hardship you are going through can lead to the good if you will turn to Him. He did that to the crippled man when He healed him. Read about the story in John 5, and you will see that Jesus even went back after he healed the man and sought him out and met with him. Do you want to get well? Then realize that you need Jesus, and turn to Him. The plan of salvation is simply this: Realize you are a sinner and that you cannot overcome this on your own. Then turn to Jesus and accept Him as Lord and Savior of your life. What then? Join a church. You cannot be saved by attending church, but Jesus loves the church and made it a powerful entity. At its very basic structure, a church is an organization of Christ-centered believers who will minister to one another and the world, allow for growth and development, and be a force of Christ-like service for change in this world—showing the world there is a better way and He is Jesus. Jesus said, "I am the way and the truth and the life." Church as God intended it is amazing and powerful, as Christ was and is.

But what if you have already accepted Christ as Lord and Savior, but you feel like you are still walking in defeat? I respectfully submit to you that you have not accepted your birthright, have not picked up your gifts, and, finally, that you are not using these gifts. What does the Bible say about the birthright of a follower of Jesus? It says you are more than a conqueror; it says that He who is in you is greater than he who is in this world; it says that you can do all things through Christ who strengthens you. The beautiful thing about it is that all the work that needed to be done for you to have victory in your life has already been done! So for you to walk in victory is simply for you to walk over ground that has already been conquered! Understand and accept that you are a child of the Most High God and that you are loved and empowered to have victory over anything that confronts you.

Can I ask you something else? Have you picked up your gifts? My wife and I have a surgeon friend who was having a baby. My wife recently got them a gift. I left the gift for him in his locker, but apparently he does not go to his locker very much because I would look back in his locker and see that it had not been picked up after two or three weeks. I even mentioned to him on several occasions that there was a gift for the baby in his locker, but he did not remember to get it. The day of the baby's arrival approached, and he still had not brought the gift home. Finally, he did bring the gift home and give it to his wife. I believe it was a baby blanket, and I hope they will use it for the baby and enjoy it. What if he had never picked up the gift and brought it home? It might have been mildly frustrating to my wife to have gone to the trouble of buying the gift if they never even bothered to unwrap it and bring it home. Perhaps more importantly, if they never brought the gift home and opened it, they would not have had the gift itself.

There is a spiritual analogy as well, from the Old Testament book of Joshua. An incredible journey of trials and tribulations but also miraculous delivery by the hand of God was reaching an end as the Jewish nation approached the Promised Land. The land was a fulfillment of a promise made by God literally hundreds of years earlier to Abraham. Joshua and the entire tribe of Israel came to an area across the Jordan River from the Promised Land and made camp. The Lord then said to Joshua, "I will give you every place where you set your foot." Then Joshua told the people, "Get your provisions ready. Three days from now you will cross the Jordan here to go in and take possession of the land the Lord your God is giving you for your own." In other words, God had a marvelous plan for the people of Israel, and it included taking them into a land of incredible prosperity. Notice the promise had been given hundreds of years earlier, but the gift had to be claimed. God said He would give the land in each place they set their foot, but what that meant was that they would have to go in to the land and claim it if they wanted it. Joshua echoed the same sentiment to the people. He recognized God had promised them the land, and he ordered them to go in and "take possession of it." If the people of Israel had never entered the Promised Land, they would not have claimed or received their gift, even though it was promised to them by God; they had to claim it to receive it. I think God may have even helped Abraham claim promises as well. At the age of seventy-five, Abraham was known as Abram. God promised, "I will make you into a great nation and I will bless you" (Genesis 12:2). But twenty-four years later, at the age of ninety-nine, Abram had still not had any children with his wife, Sarah. What did God do? He changed the man's name to Abraham, which literally means in Hebrew "father of a multitude." So any time anyone would call on Abraham, they were reminding the patriarch of God's promise. One year later, at the age of one hundred, Abraham and Sarah had their first child, Isaac, whose children went on to form the entire tribe of Israel. I wonder how many times Abraham spoke his name or had his name spoken to him, resulting in the claiming of God's gift.

We now live under a new covenant. Jesus has come and redeemed us from sin and death, offering us eternal life. Those who have accepted Jesus as Lord and Savior have the indwelling Holy Spirit to guide, counsel, and empower them. We also have what I believe is a sometimes overlooked but incredibly powerful aid to us in the holy scripture and the promises it contains. These promises are incredible and certainly no less than those given to Abraham hundreds of years ago. Listen to this: "His divine power has given us everything we need for a godly life through our knowledge of Him who called us by His own glory and goodness. Through these He has given us His very great and precious promises, so that through them you may participate in the divine nature" (2 Peter 1:4). The Bible talks about Jesus and those who believe in Him, saying, "In this world we are like Him" (1 John 4:17). There are literally hundreds of promises for us in scripture to encourage and empower us; they literally allow us to participate in the "divine nature." There are some really incredible promises. God promised the people of Israel the Promised Land hundreds of years before they arrived in the area. The land would be given as "every place they set their feet." The promises of the Bible are "great and precious." Have you gone by and claimed them for your life? You may be overlooking something that was meant to bring you victory. Do you feel like maybe some or even most of the promises in scripture are not meant for you? The Bible says, "For no matter how many promises God has made, they are 'Yes' in Christ.

And so through Him the 'Amen' is spoken by us to the glory of God" (2 Corinthians 1:20). All the promises God has made are lying right there in your Bible for you to claim and use for incredible victory in your life. Claim them! Use them! If you think the promises in the Bible have somehow expired and are not for you, consider the following verse: "And you are heirs of the prophets and of the covenant God made with your fathers" (Acts 3:24).

A final question: Do you have gifts you may have been given and even possess but are not using? If you got a lawn mower for a gift, and even went by and picked it up, unless you use it, it won't do any good. Your yard will not get mowed if you are sitting on the couch and the mower is in the shed not being used. There is something in addition to the incredible promises in scripture that we have been given that is extremely powerful and that we already have but very few people use. Most people do not use it simply because they don't understand the full depths of this gift. What is this gift? It is authority. In the spiritual realm, authority is critically important. Consider the story of Adam and Eve. On the surface, it just seems pretty severe to suggest that eating the "wrong" fruit would have somehow launched mankind on a path of sin, hardship, and death when God's original intention was to have them live and work in the Garden of Eden in perfect bliss. What happened, though, was all about authority; Adam and Eve rejected the instructions of God and His authority and followed the advice of Satan, the serpent, submitting themselves and mankind to his authority. Thankfully, Jesus redeemed us from this slavery to death and reestablished our birthright as sons and daughters of God. Plain and simple, we have been given an enormous amount of power and authority on earth, and we are to use it to reign as kings on this earth. This is contrary to what many might believe. Many Christians believe we have to live on this earth constantly being beat up by the devil and the world, with the whole idea that things will be much better when we get to heaven. Make no mistake, heaven will be wonderful, but the Bible never says a follower of Christ has to walk in defeat on earth. Scripture actually says quite the contrary; we are to "reign" in our lives on earth, much as a king would reign in his kingdom. Scripture says, "How much more will those who receive God's abundant provision of grace and of the gift of righteousness reign in life through the one man, Jesus Christ" (Romans 5:17). Scripture says we have been raised with Christ to reign right now: "And God raised us up with Christ and seated us with Him in the heavenly realms in Christ Jesus" (Ephesians 2:6). Does the Bible really say we have authority to live in victory here on earth? Absolutely! The Bible says, "I have given you authority to trample on snakes and scorpions and to overcome all the power of the enemy, nothing will harm you" (Luke 10:18). If you have been given authority, but you don't use it or even know about it, it is pretty much worthless to you. Authority is only useful if you use it. Is it really possible we could be missing something so simple but also so critical for living in victory? Unfortunately, yes. As the Bible says, "My people are destroyed for lack of knowledge" (Hosea 4:6). The apostles themselves are good examples of this. They had a tremendous ministry to heal the sick. In some cases, sick people would be placed out in the street, and the shadows of the apostles passing over them would cure them, or even a cloth they had touched could be used. Despite the many miracles they performed, there is no healing miracle recorded in the New Testament after the ascension of Jesus in which the apostles prayed to Jesus for Him to heal the sick person. They simply and powerfully used the name of Jesus and the authority they already had been given to heal the sick. Are there examples in the Bible before this, when the apostles did not understand they had authority and so failed to use it? I believe so. We all know the story in Matthew 8, but take a moment to consider what it says about spiritual authority. The disciples followed Jesus on to a boat and went out into the water. A great storm came up that was so severe it threatened to engulf the boat. The disciples went to Jesus (who was sleeping) and asked that He save them. Jesus got up and asked, "You of little faith, why are you so afraid?" He then rebuked the wind and waves, the storm quieted, and they got to their destination. Notice one thing. The disciples did not lack faith in Jesus. When the storm came, they went right to Jesus, knowing He could deliver them. What they did not have faith in, however, was the authority they had been given and their own ability to rebuke and calm the storm. There is a somewhat similar theme in Matthew 17, when the apostles come to Jesus to heal a boy, and He rebukes the apostles first and then heals the boy. "How long shall I put up with you?" Jesus laments. Again, in this story, it is not a lack of faith they have in Jesus, because they come to Him to heal the boy; it is the lack of understanding that they have to exercise their own authority to heal the boy that seems to frustrate Jesus. Can you imagine giving someone everything they need to achieve victory and then not having them use it or even recognize that they have it? Thankfully, by the book of Acts, the apostles clearly understand and use the spiritual authority they do have.

Healing Grace

We have this authority as well, as promised to us in the holy scripture. I believe there is even an example of this in the Old Testament. God gave Moses authority. When the Egyptian army was pursuing Israel and had cornered the fleeing Israelites, the Hebrews became terrified, and Moses cried out to the Lord. What did the Lord say? "Why are you crying out to me? Tell the Israelites to move on. Raise your staff and stretch out your hand over the sea to divide the water so that the Israelites can go through dry ground" (Exodus 14:15). Moses did not lack faith in God but rather seemed not fully to appreciate the degree of spiritual authority and tools he had been given to defeat Egypt. If you doubt that believers today have this powerful authority to even do the miraculous, consider what Jesus said in John 14: "Very truly I tell you, whoever believes in me will do the works I have been doing, and they will do even greater works than these because I am going to the Father. And I will do whatever you ask in my name, so that the Father may be glorified in the Son." Jesus said that after He had walked on water, healed the sick, and raised the dead—we would be able to do even greater things than these. Now that is authority!

Imagine you are a student in a high school and one of the classes you are taking is called Study Room. It is simply a time for students to study quietly in preparation for their other classes. Due to cutbacks, the study room teacher is laid off, and so the school compensates for this by appointing the students themselves to rotate as study room teachers. To maintain order, these student teachers are given authority to discipline or even expel students if they become unruly in the study room. One day you go to study room and have a lot of work to do. You are looking forward to being productive, getting a lot of things done, and are grateful for the time to do it. But when you get in the study room, it is chaos. People are being loud, running all over, and even throwing things, and there does not seem to be anyone in charge; you are not able to get any work done. You even try to get them to stop, but no one pays any attention to you. Suddenly you realize that this is the day you are assigned to be the study room teacher! You quickly get up, walk to the head of the class, rebuke the unruly students, quickly restore order, and then you are finally able to get your work done. What happened? Well, you realized and accepted the authority which had been given to you and used it as it was meant to be used. If you had never realized and never used the authority you had available to you, the chaos around you probably would have continued. We absolutely have an enormous amount of God-given authority here on earth for us to use.

To summarize this section, particularly for someone going through hardship, I believe God has already given us everything we need to live in complete victory right here and right now on earth. We have Jesus, we have the Holy Spirit, we have the holy scripture in which God has given us extraordinary promises to claim and use, and finally, we have authority over anything that confronts us. I believe the biblical advice for someone going through physical hardship is to really get in the scripture and look for the gifts He has given you and then claim them for your life. They are intended for you, they are your birthright, and they are there for you to claim and to empower you. I resisted the notion I could just list all of the promises God makes in the Bible, because I do not think that is what God has in mind for you as a reader of this book. There are literally hundreds of promises, spread throughout scripture; but to learn them all, you must read the Bible regularly and completely, and in so doing, you will develop more of a daily relationship and appreciation for Him. He wants a relationship with you! When the nation of Israel came to the Promised Land, God agreed to give it "little by little." He wants you to individually set your feet on the Promised Land of the holy scripture and find and claim these promises for your life. Not to internalize these promises and claim them for your life is to miss out on some great and precious gifts God has intended for you. I could not resist listing a small portion of my favorite promises that I claim for my life below, but it is certainly not complete. Finally, realize (and research if you need to) the spiritual authority you have been given for right now in Jesus Christ. I really do believe He wants you to live a life in complete and total victory. Why would He send His Son to die for your sins to have you live in defeat? I believe He purposely has given us promises in scripture as gifts that must be claimed but will then allow us to live in the victorious life He intended.

Do you want to be well? Claim your birthright! Pick up your gifts and claim your promises! Use your authority! I end this section with some promises I claim for myself, and also with Psalm 91, which is mostly comprised of promises for us, particularly for those going through hardship:

> He who dwells in the shelter of the Most High will rest in the shadow of the Almighty. I will say of the Lord, surely He will save you from the fowler's snare and from deadly pestilence. He will cover you with His feathers, and under His wings you will find refuge; His faithfulness will be your shield and rampart.

You will not fear the terror of night, nor the arrow that flies by day, nor the pestilence that stalks in the darkness, nor the plague that destroys at midday. A thousand may fall at your side, ten thousand at your right hand, but it will not come near you. You will only observe with your eyes and see the punishment of the wicked. If you make the Most High your dwelling—even the Lord, who is my refuge—then no harm will befall you, no disaster will come near your tent. For He will command His angels concerning you to guard you in all your ways; they will lift you up in their hands, so that you will not strike your foot against a stone. You will tread upon the lion and the cobra; you will trample the great lion and the serpent. "Because he loves me," says the Lord, "I will rescue him; I will protect him because he acknowledges my name. He will call upon me, and I will answer him; I will be with him in trouble, I will deliver him and honor him. With long life will I satisfy him and show him my salvation." (Psalm 91)

Here are some of my favorite promises in scripture, which I claim for myself and my family:

I am fearfully and wonderfully made.
—Psalm 139

I walk in divine health.
—Proverbs 3

I can do anything through Christ who strengthens me.
—Philippians 4

He who is in me is greater than he who is in this world.
—1 John

God has a plan for me.
—Jeremiah 29

I have been healed.
—1 Peter

I have been forgiven.
—Psalm 103

Edward W. Hellman, M.D.

I am blessed.
—Matthew 5

I am redeemed.
—Galatians 3

I am saved.
—Romans 10

I will receive what I ask God for.
—Mark 7

I am made in God's image and likeness.
—Genesis 1

I have authority over anything in this world that confronts me.
—Luke 10

I am more than a conqueror.
—Romans 8

I can do the miraculous.
—John 14

I have the Kingdom of God inside me.
—Luke 17

God gave me a spirit of power, love, and self-discipline.
—2 Timothy 1

I have the Holy Spirit inside me.
—Luke 12

I have angels that serve me.
—Hebrews 1

God will never leave me or forsake me.
—Joshua 1

God has prepared great things for me.
—John 14

No weapon formed against me will prosper.
—Isaiah 54:17

No disaster, sickness or disease will come near my tent.
—Psalm 91:10

Everything I put my hand to will be blessed.
-- Deuteronomy 28:8

Thank You, Lord, that You have given us so many great promises in scripture and such great authority to live in victory here on earth!

I challenge you to make a list of all the promises in the Bible that you would like to claim for your life. And remember that on a great day, or even on a really bad day—maybe even the worst day you have had in your whole life—God is there, and He is faithful, and His promises and commitment to you and His love for you do not change. As the Bible says, His promises are precious and allow us to participate in the divine nature. All His promises are yes and amen to us. His promises are for you; He has made a covenant with you.

You were born to be awesome and to live in victory. Just do it! Claim and use the promises that are waiting for you!

6) CHOOSE LIFE—WIN YOUR BATTLE

In a previous section, we talked about the importance of understanding and appreciating the incredible power of the grace and mercy of our Lord Jesus Christ, which I truly believe with all my heart. Before I was ever born, Jesus came down in the flesh as God and man. He redeemed me from sin and death, offering me and others like me the chance of eternal life if we would just believe in Him. Every work that needed to be done has been done for me to achieve complete and total victory. By His stripes, we were healed from sickness and death. We have been given Jesus, to intercede on our behalf as He sits at the right hand of God the Father; we have been given the Holy Spirit to counsel and empower us; we have been given powerful angels to serve us; we have been given the holy scripture to guide and further empower us; we have been given fellow believers and the powerful church to further enable and disciple us. As I have said before and will say again, victory is ours and has already been won for us. The Christian who walks in victory is simply walking on ground that has already been conquered long ago!

So it may seem contradictory to say there is a battle all around you, and it is something you would do well to win—and only you can win it. It is not the war between God and Satan—that has already taken place and has already been decided. The battle, simply put, is over your heart and mind. God has provided you the opportunity to walk in victory, but that does not mean you will do so. You see, God could have made things easy. He could have made us as robots, programmed to be obedient, worship Him, and even to be incredibly happy. Life might have been simpler, but where is the love in that? The very essence of God is love. And love ultimately involves a freedom of will—the freedom to love God or to reject Him. The battle I am speaking about may seem very small. It is about your free will and how you will use it this very day. What will you choose to think and meditate about, what will you put your faith and trust in today, what will you choose to speak about, and how will you treat people today? What you have placed your faith in today, what you believe in, what you choose to meditate on and think over, the words you speak, and the way you treat others will greatly influence whether you live in victory for yourself and others or live in defeat today. And as much as God loves you, He will not control you. And as much as the devil hates you and all Christians, he will try to frustrate you and make you unfruitful today. The battle over what you choose to believe and think about and what you put your faith in is a battle only you can win for yourself.

How do you win your battle to live in victory? First, you must understand that it is a battle. The biggest lie of the devil is the idea that he does not even exist. The Bible speaks differently, recommending to believers, "Be self-controlled and alert. Your enemy the devil prowls around like a roaring lion looking for someone to devour" (1 Peter 5:8). That does not mean you should be afraid, because the Bible also says that if we resist him, he will flee from us, and that we are "more than conquerors," but you should have an understanding that the devil does exist and that he may try to influence you and those around you. Second, understand that everything about what you do and say ultimately stems from your thoughts and your beliefs. So make sure that what you believe in is the truth and not a deception, and be careful what you choose to spend your time thinking about. That is the battleground of your day; what you choose to believe in and what you choose to think about will affect your mood, your words, your acts, how you feel, and how you treat others. It will also determine the nature of the fruit you produce. Like a garden, the words we say and the actions we put out there to others will either bear good fruit or thorns and bristles; we will either be a source of hope and encouragement or a source of discouragement. Our words and actions always will stem from our beliefs and thoughts. It is impossible for them to be at odds. You may be able to fake them for a while, but they will ultimately reveal your heart. As the Bible says, "Can both fresh water and salt water flow from the same spring? My brothers, can a fig tree bear olives, or a grapevine bear figs? Neither can a salt spring produce fresh water" (James 3:11). It is highly unlikely you could be believing and having your thoughts dwell on something negative and be a source of encouragement, or be dwelling on something positive and be a source of discouragement.

What must you do then, for yourselves and for others? Choose life! Consider this scripture:

> This day I call heaven and earth as witnesses against you that I have set before you life and death, blessings and curses. Now choose life, so that you may love the Lord your God, listen to His voice, and hold fast to Him. For the Lord is your life. (Deuteronomy 30:19–20)

Edward W. Hellman, M.D.

Winning your own daily battle and choosing life is as simple as making sure the meditations of your heart are in good relationship with God throughout the day. As the Bible says, "Be joyful always; pray continually; give thanks in all circumstances, for this is God's will for you in Christ Jesus" (1 Thessalonians 5:16). That is pretty profound. Many people spend their whole lives seeking God's will for them, and there it is right there! And notice it all involves the meditations of your heart and your thought life. If you are always joyful, always thankful, and continually praying, your heart will be continually meditating on God, and you will be a source of encouragement to others. If you choose to continually meditate on things that are negative and sinful and destructive, it is unlikely you will be a source for much encouragement to others. As Bill Johnson, pastor of Bethel Church in Redding, California, puts it: "I cannot afford to have a thought in my head about me that is not in His." That is your battle that only you can win. Paul describes this battle very well in this scripture: "For though we live in the world, we do not wage war as the world does. The weapons we fight with are not the weapons of the world. On the contrary, they have divine power to demolish strongholds. We demolish arguments and every pretension that sets itself up against the knowledge of God, and we take captive every thought to make it obedient to Christ" (2 Corinthians 10:3-5). Even more profound! We have divine power to demolish strongholds! How do we do that? We take captive every thought we have and make it obedient to Christ! Consider the people who are discouraged and hopeless because of the hardships they are going through, in part because they believe the lies of Satan. What if something happens in their interaction with you, and they leave with hope and encouragement that then grows into faith in Christ that then grows into Christian love? You talk about demolishing a stronghold for that person! I submit to you it all begins with your daily decision and pattern regarding what you are going to spend your day believing in and meditating on; that is your battle. It takes some discipline to control your meditations and your thought life, but remember that God gave us "a spirit of power, love, and self-discipline" (2 Timothy 1:7).

Consider it another way. Would it not be incredible if we could be totally transformed today? The Bible says we can be: "Do not conform any longer to the pattern of this world, but be transformed by the renewing of your mind" (Romans 12:2). Renewing your mind and what you think about can literally transform you! Where the pattern of the world is discouragement and hopelessness, "the fruit of the Spirit is love, joy, peace, patience, kindness, goodness, faithfulness, gentleness, and self-control. Against such things there is no law" (Galatians 5:22-23). How do we attain this? Again, it is through our thought life, what we believe and choose to meditate on during our day. Consider the consequences of continually meditating and being thankful for God and His glory: "And we, who with unveiled faces all reflect the Lord's glory, are being transformed into His likeness with ever-increasing glory, which comes from the Lord, who is the Spirit" (2 Corinthians 3:18). In other words, as we chose to believe in and meditate on the very nature and glory of God, we are literally being transformed ourselves, even into His likeness! Wow! I like the American King James translation of Proverbs 27:3, which says, "For as he thinks in his heart, so is he."

Another component to guarding your thought life is managing your environment. The environment you are in can absolutely affect your thought life, for the better or the worse. The Bible says, "Bad company corrupts good character" (1 Corinthians 15:33), referring to the possibility that being around people who regularly reject God's ways by their actions and behavior can negatively affect your own character; similarly, "He who walks with the wise grows wise, but a companion of fools suffers harm" (Proverbs 13:20). Proverbs 22:24 says something similar: "Do not make friends with a hot tempered man, do not associate with one easily angered, or you may learn his ways and get yourself ensnared." This is very much an issue in the spiritual realms as well; scripture says, "You cannot drink the cup of the Lord and the cup of demons too; you cannot have a part in both the Lord's table and the table of demons" (1 Corinthians 10:21). On the other hand, being around people of godly character can really strengthen and encourage you. On that topic, scripture says, "As iron sharpens iron, so one man sharpens another" (Proverbs 27:17). I think the environment around you can also have an effect on your healing; the Bible alludes to it. Look if you will at the story of Jesus healing a blind man, told in Mark 8:22, in the town of Bethsaida. Bethsaida was a town that was chastised by Jesus for its lack of faith. As Jesus said, "Woe to you, Bethsaida! If the miracles that were performed in you had been performed in Tyre and Sidon, they would have repented long ago in sackcloth and ashes. But I tell you, it will be more bearable for Tyre and Sidon on the Day of Judgment than for you" (Matthew 11:21-22). So back to Jesus and the blind man in Bethsaida. What is the first thing Jesus does with the man before He heals him? He leads the blind man out of town. And what does Jesus say to the blind man after He restores the blind man's sight? Jesus tells the man not to go back to Bethsaida. Consider the following scripture: "For what do righteousness and wickedness have in common? Or what fellowship can light have with darkness? What harmony is there between Christ and Belial? What does a believer have in common with an unbeliever? What agreement is there between the temple of God and idols? For we are a temple of the living God" (2 Corinthians 6:14-16).

I submit to you that you do have a lot of control in managing your environment. While it is probably a good idea to stay reasonably informed, television can provide a never-ending litany of negative influence. You simply don't have to spend all day, in my opinion, listening to the never-ending stories about conspiracy theories, corruption, and crime; the same thing for music, newspapers, magazines, and movies. It helps to understand the times, but by listening to the never-ending stream of negative information, you can become negatively influenced by your environment. Why would you want to waste any time surrounding yourself with things that are not uplifting or honoring to God? It can really affect the nature of what you are thinking about on any particular day. But what about the times you might feel like you have no control over the environment you are in? Is it possible to manage your environment if you work in a hostile office, or you are a patient in a hospital, or you are bedridden in a nursing home? I submit to you the answer is yes, but it might take some discipline and conscious decision making on your part. It really comes down to how you choose to see things. You can be thankful or complain regarding just about anything. Basically, you will find what you are looking for. I have a friend, Charles Gustkey, who gave a good example of this. You buy a Honda minivan, and then you start noticing how many other Honda minivans are on the road. It is because you are now looking for them. You found them because you are looking for them. When you were not looking for them, you probably did not notice them. If you look for the good in people and your situation, you will find it. But the same person with the same situation but a different attitude can find the bad in anything. Paul was a great example of this. Much of his writings were from prison. In one account in the book of Acts, he had been stripped and severely flogged, and an angel came to rescue him and Silas at midnight. The angel found them praying and singing hymns to God! And the other prisoners were listening as well; what a testimony! The Bible describes it like this: "The eye is the lamp of the body. If your eyes are good, your whole body will be full of light. But if your eyes are bad, your whole body will be full of darkness" (Matthew 6:22). So, if you will make a conscious decision to see the good, your whole body will be full of light, which I believe will lead to a spirit of joy and thankfulness, which is incredibly powerful in healing. As the Bible says, "A cheerful heart is good medicine, but a crushed spirit dries up the bones" (Proverbs 17:22). Choose a cheerful heart!

Finally, it has become increasingly supported by research that your thought life can have profound medical implications. Every thought you have and then subsequently choose to meditate on is associated with some physiologic response in your body. When you choose to meditate on all the stressful, negative things you are going through, it creates a stress-like response in which a steroid is secreted by the body in what is known as a flight-or-fight response. Repetitive exposure to steroids in high doses suppresses your immune system, raises your blood pressure, elevates your blood sugar, decreases the protective layer of mucus in the stomach, causes osteoporosis, and increases cancer risk, among many other negative health impacts. Every time your thoughts return to that event, the physiologic response occurs. Meditating on positive things leads to the secretion of pleasurable endorphins, which lower blood pressure and leave a person with a feeling of peace and well-being. Your thoughts are literally creating a chemical bath, which your body is continually immersed in, whether good or bad. It has been shown that thinking positive thoughts can actually change some of the neuron pathways in your brain. Chronic patterns in negative thinking can lead to chronic physiologic changes in your body that can endanger your very health.

In summary, I believe the Bible encourages a person going through hardship to really take a step back and make a commitment to win his or her own battle—not the battle of salvation, which has been offered to us as a gift, but the battle of what we will choose to believe and meditate on in our thought life each and every day. This will affect our lives, our health, our relationships, and the amount of fruit we bear in our lives. Simply put, it is God's will for our lives to be joyful, thankful, and in continuous prayer with Him. As the Bible says, "the joy of the Lord is your strength" (Nehemiah 8:10). I end this section with a verse from the book of Philippians and encourage you to claim it for victory in the battles of your life.

> Rejoice in the Lord always, I will say it again: Rejoice! Let your gentleness be evident to all. The Lord is near. Do not be anxious

about anything, but in everything, by prayer and petition, with thanksgiving, present your requests to God. And the peace of God, which transcends all understanding, will guard your hearts and your minds in Christ Jesus. Finally, brothers, whatever is true, whatever is noble, whatever is right, whatever is pure, whatever is lovely, whatever is admirable—if anything is excellent or praiseworthy—think about such things. Whatever you have learned or received or heard from me, or seen in me—put into practice. And the God of peace will be with you. (Philippians 4:4–9)

I love the prayer that David prayed in Psalm 139. This is the same David who was chased by Saul, who was trying to kill him—the same David whose son chased him out of town and was trying to kill him. This is what David prayed: "Search me, God, and know my heart; test me and know my anxious thoughts. See if there is any offensive way in me, and lead me in the way everlasting" (Psalm 139:23-24). David was not asking for help getting revenge on those who were trying to persecute and kill him; he was asking for help with a battle he knew was very important, the meditations of his heart and his thought life. We should do the same. David also wrote one of my favorite verses in the whole Bible; it speaks to a similar theme:

I will sing to the Lord all my life; I will sing praise to my God as long as I live. May my meditation be pleasing to Him, as I rejoice in the Lord. (Psalm 104:33–34)

7) FIGHT LIKE A SUPERHERO—GIVE LIFE

> Be strong and let us fight bravely for our people and the cities of our God. The Lord will do what is good in His sight.
> —2 Samuel 10:12

Have you heard about superheroes? What makes someone a superhero is the ability to do at least one thing far above and beyond the normal. These heroes uniformly use their abilities to fight for justice and the common man. Superman could fly through the air and had superhuman strength. Flash was incredibly fast. Aquaman could swim through the waters and communicate with fish. There is even a superhero named Antman who could shrink to the size of an ant and talk to insects. You know what I think? Jesus is the ultimate superhero! He can walk on water, turn water into wine, heal the sick, cast out demons, fly into the heavens, and raise people from the dead. He is truly the best superhero of all time. You know who else is a superhero? You are! How do I know that? Jesus said it. If you accept that Jesus is a superhero, then consider what He said in John 14: "I tell you the truth, anyone who has faith in me will do whatever I have been doing. He will do even greater things than these, because I am going to the Father. And I will do whatever you ask in my name, so that the Son may bring glory to the Father. You may ask me for anything in my name, and I will do it" (John 14:12–14). That is right; Jesus said you will be capable of accomplishing more than He did after He ascended into heaven. But what if you were a superhero and did not know it, or what if you had super powers but were not using them correctly, or even using them at all?

Do you still doubt you are a superhero? Consider what the Bible says about a follower of Jesus. Jesus said you will be filled with the Holy Spirit. The presence of God will literally reside inside you to counsel you and empower you. The Bible says we will have angels to serve us. As in the scripture above in John 14 and many others, Jesus says He will be seated at the right hand of God the Father and will intervene for us, giving us what we ask for in His name. We have the incredible resource of the holy scripture to guide us, but also with it, we have God's powerful promises for our lives. We also have the church itself, the fellowship of disciples in Christ whom Christ loves and has empowered.

So if you are a superhero, what is your superpower? I respectively submit to you that among your superpowers is the power of the words you speak. With our words, we can curse or bless, we can build up or tear down, we can give hope or take it away. I believe the words we say can have an important impact on the healing and health of others and ourselves. Do you doubt that the words you speak have tremendous power? Listen to what scripture says about it: "The tongue has the power of life and death, and those who love it will eat of its fruit" (Proverbs 18:21). Life and death? Sounds pretty powerful to me. If we really believed we have power and authority in the spiritual realms, we need to be extremely careful and give full consideration to what we say, just as you would be careful in how you use a powerful weapon. You would not play around with a loaded gun; you would be careful with it and make sure it was used only for good. Otherwise someone might get hurt. The Bible emphasizes this idea on many occasions; one of the most profound, I believe, is this: "If anyone speaks, he should do it as one speaking the very words of God. If anyone serves, they should do so with the strength God provides, so that in all things God may be praised through Jesus Christ. To Him be the glory and the power for ever and ever. Amen" (1 Peter 4:11). Well-spoken words of encouragement and wisdom can be such an incredibly powerful thing; they can literally give life and health. As the Bible says, "A wholesome tongue is a tree of life" (Proverbs 15:4), and, "Pleasant words are a honeycomb, sweet to the soul and healing to the bones" (Proverbs 16:24).

I commend those who routinely use the power of their words to build themselves and others up. The ability to use our words to encourage others may seem like a small thing, but I submit to you that by taking a person who is discouraged and giving him or her hope, you are literally destroying strongholds and creating rejoicing in heaven by putting that person on a better path. I will tell you that in my practice and my life in general, I have heard people inadvertently curse themselves and others. Is that really possible? I know it may sound silly to you, but if you believe you have spiritual power and authority, think about some of the things people will say: "Now that I am fifty, my body is falling apart"; "I am eaten up with arthritis"; "I am sick"; "I am tired"; "I am clumsy"; "I am beat"; "Nothing good ever happens to me"; even something simple like, "I get a bad cold every year" (guess what, they usually do!). What we say can have spiritual and physical implications. What really makes me shudder is when I believe someone inadvertently curses their children; for example, they'll say something like, "He never does anything right" or "She is always sick." When someone says something like that in front of me, I take a stand against it. Again, I understand some people might think it is silly. But I submit to you that if you really believe you are a child of God and empowered by the promises of the Bible, you will be extremely careful and thoughtful about what you say. You will consider your ability to speak as a superpower.

I submit to you that you and your place are important in the kingdom of God and that much of your impact will revolve around the words you speak. Consider the following verse: "We are therefore Christ's ambassadors, as though God were making his appeal through us. We implore you on Christ's behalf; be reconciled to God" (2 Corinthians 5:20). I believe the Bible encourages those going through hardship—and in fact everyone in general—to really consider the words we speak as something that does have a real degree of power. People should use their words to build themselves and others up and, in doing so, be a blessing to themselves and others, building up the church and bringing glory to God; as the Bible says, "I urge you to live a life worthy of the calling you have received. Be completely humble and gentle; be patient, bearing with one another in love. Make every effort to keep the unity of the Spirit through the bond of peace" (Ephesians 4:1-3).

Mother Theresa was a well-known figure who inspired many by her acts of service and love for the orphans and poor in India. One of her more memorable recommendations that stuck in my mind was to "do small things with great love." The Bible says something I think is similar: "So whether you eat or drink or whatever you do, do it all for the glory of God" (1 Corinthians 10:31). I think that is such good advice. You can know all the scripture verses and sermons and facts about the Bible that there are, but it is ultimately God's love that changes the world. The world needs the love of Jesus, and reaching the world can begin with a small act. There is an expression, originally spoken by Theodore Roosevelt, who said, "No one cares how much you know, until they know how much you care." Giving encouragement to others by your words and actions can open the door for a relationship with Jesus for them. Now that is a superpower! The Bible says there is actually rejoicing in heaven when a sinner repents to follow Jesus! Be a superhero! Give life to yourself and others with your words.

Edward W. Hellman, M.D.

May our Lord Jesus Christ Himself and God our Father, who loved us and by His grace gave us eternal encouragement and good hope, encourage your hearts and strengthen you in every good deed and word. (1 Thessalonians 2:16–17)

8) PRAISE

I will sing to the Lord all my life; I will sing praise to my God as long as I live. May my meditation be pleasing to Him, as I rejoice in the Lord.
—Psalm 104:33-34

Blessed are those who have learned to acclaim you, who walk in the light of your presence, O Lord. They rejoice in your name all day long; they exult in your righteousness. For you are their glory and strength, and by your favor you exalt our horn.
—Psalm 89:15-17

I have seen you in the sanctuary and beheld your power and your glory. Because your love is better than life, I will praise you as long as I live, and in your name I will lift up my hands. My soul will be satisfied as with the richest of foods; with singing lips my mouth will praise you.
—Psalm 63:2-5

O Lord, you are my God; I will exalt you and praise your name, for in perfect faithfulness you have done marvelous things, things planned long ago.
—Isaiah 25:1

Imagine getting an expensive gift but then not knowing quite how to use it properly. Maybe worse, you look through the box and don't find an owner's manual or any set of instructions. I admit that when my wife and I got married, we got a few gifts that I absolutely had no idea how to use—mostly kitchen stuff. I bring this up to say the obvious—that for a device to work at peak performance, you have to use it in the manner for which it was designed. For example, a blender would make a pretty poor lawn mower, and it would be difficult (and messy) to try to make Brunswick stew in a washing machine.

Edward W. Hellman, M.D.

What am I getting at? When we were created, it was for a purpose or purposes. And I feel with all my heart that one of the reasons I was created was to praise and worship God. I totally sense in my spirit that when I let go of everything else and am totally lost in praising and worshipping God, I am coming completely in line with His purpose for me—like a car firing on all cylinders but so much more. It may be at a worship service at church, at a concert, alone in the car, or in surgery; I just feel that if I could stay as totally connected to God as I am at that moment, everything would be okay. And it is not about the music; sometimes it is seeing a beautiful sunrise and praising God; sometimes it is seeing a miraculous healing or an act of courage.

There is something about an object of creation functioning for the purpose it was intended that speaks to divine performance and health. On the other hand, you can tear up an object of creation if it was not used in the manner intended. Try mixing cement in your blender! If we have somehow spiritually and physically torn up our bodies by living in contradiction to the reason we were created, I submit to you it is never too late to get back on track. And the simplest way to do this is to start immediately praising and worshipping God! Simply put, praising God will get your heart and soul back in line with its originally intended purpose; divine health will soon follow.

I think the followers of Jesus must have noticed something very different about the way He prayed. For one thing, He did not seem to do it in the long and attention-getting way the chief priests of the day did; and secondly, His prayers were accompanied by enormous power. So His disciples asked Jesus to show them how to pray. It should not be lost that when Jesus did teach the disciples what has become known as the Lord's Prayer, the first part of the prayer is pure praise: "Our Father, who art in heaven, hallowed be they name." Praise is the first thing that should come out of any attempt to communicate with God. The Bible talks about our prayers rising up as fragrant offerings to God in heaven.

I submit to you that there is no problem you will ever face that cannot be completely overcome by simply turning your heart to praising and worshipping God. If you continuously praise and worship God, there is simply no room for anything else; everything else simply gets pushed out. This is completely different from trying to overcome something by your own strength. In Matthew 12:43, Jesus talks about a man who is possessed by an evil spirit. For whatever reason, the spirit leaves, and the man gets his life together and cleans up his act. But scripture says that the spirit comes back and finds everything clean, in order, and *unoccupied*. It returns with seven other spirits with it, making the man's final condition worse than it was to begin with. Note the term *unoccupied*. The man living in his own strength had no ability to withstand the evil spirits. How many times have we seen it? A drug addict enters rehab, cleans up his act, but then returns to his addiction, often worse than he ever was, sometimes ending up in a tragic overdose. He relied on his own strength. Jesus tells about another way to be rid of evil spirits. In the same story but told in Luke, Jesus said, "If I drive out demons by the finger of God, then the kingdom of God has come to you." Have you ever noticed the difference? An addict who gets cleaned up of his or her own power is still an addict and must always go around fighting that urge to use cocaine or whatever the addiction is for the rest of his life; that is why it is so hard to stay clean. But have you ever met an addict who was delivered from it through Jesus? They say they have absolutely no desire for the addiction. Can you imagine a spirit trying to enter a man who has the very kingdom of God inside him? It simply will not and cannot happen. Their spirit is so full with praise and worship and the very kingdom of God that there is simply no room for anything else! For a visual image of this, imagine a feather (your problem) resting in an empty bowl (your spirit). The feather floats away, but then returns later with seven other feathers to reoccupy the bowl. Now imagine a feather resting in an empty bowl that gets completely filled with water, even to the point of overflowing. That feather has been sent from the bowl, and there simply is not any room for it to ever return. John 7:37 says, "If anyone is thirsty, let him come to me and drink. Whoever believes in me, as the Scripture has said, streams of living water will flow from within him." The Bible says not only that the joy of the Lord is our strength (Nehemiah 8:10) but that rejoicing in the Lord is actually a "safeguard" for us (Philippians 3:1).

What is the thing you would like to get rid of? Is it anxiety, anger, greed, frustration, an addiction? If we live under our own strength, we are unoccupied, empty houses that will ultimately be filled with something. A void in nature is ultimately filled with something. Fear is a good example. One of my favorite movies of all time is *Facing the Giants*, in which the members of a struggling football team commit themselves to God and become excellent in what they do, even winning a state championship. In the movie, Mark Richt, the University of Georgia football coach, makes a cameo appearance and has a line that I think is quite profound. He says that the Bible says the equivalent of "do not fear" 365 times. Isn't that interesting? One for every single day of the year! How can we get rid of things we don't want in our lives? Don't focus on the condition. What does it mean to wash out something? It means to introduce water and a cleansing agent into the dirty area until there is no longer any room for the dirt. Do you want to overcome a drug addiction? Don't go around thinking over and over about how you are no longer going to take the drug. That usually does not work, because it keeps the problem on your mind. Fill yourself so full of praise for Jesus there is no room for anything else.

It does not have to be drugs. What is your hardship, your obstacle, your fear? Can you take a moment and just put it aside? Can you forget everything about yourself and completely give every single part of your entire body over to praising and worshipping Jesus? One of the hardest things to do when you are going through a hardship is to take the focus off yourself, and yet it is one of the most critical things to do to overcome it. But can you find one thing that will help you to totally and recklessly forget about yourself in this very moment and focus on Jesus? It may be a song. It may be a memory of how God delivered you or someone you know. It may be something from nature, a scripture, or a worship song. Find that place in your heart where you can go to and praise Jesus as you were created to do and as He so much deserves. And as the moments turn into minutes and hopefully hours, don't go back. Continually think about more and more ways in which you can praise and worship Jesus. And you know what? All those problems you thought you had will take care of themselves. Life is too short not to spend every moment with Jesus, praising Him. If you are really going through a hardship and you want to be transformed, drop everything you are doing and praise and worship Jesus, and never go back. Don't waste any more time while you are here on earth doing anything else. As you come in line with God's very purpose for your life, divine health will flow from you.

Bitterness, lack of forgiveness, hostility, and so many negative emotions are at the root of multiple physical ailments, maybe even the majority of them; when someone is absorbed in praising God, there simply isn't any room for any of these negative emotions or their negative health consequences. The Israelites were in the desert and came to a body of water that was called Marah, which literally means bitter. The Israelites could not drink the water, or they would become ill. What did God do? He turned the bitter water into sweet water. What did He say? "I am the

Healing Grace

God who Heals you" (Exodus 15:26). Exchanging a spirit that is bitter for one that is absorbed in praising God can heal you! Turn any bitterness or unforgiveness you may have into praise! When we are totally absorbed in praising God, I think we really begin to get a fuller appreciation and understanding of God's incredible love for us. What happens then? "I pray that you, being rooted and established in love, may have the power, together with all of God's holy people, to grasp how long and wide and high and deep is the love of Christ, and to know this love that surpasses knowledge—that you may be filled to the measure of all the fullness of God" (Ephesians 3:17-19). Could there really be anything better than to be filled with the fullness of God?

Praise has two very close relatives that are also extremely powerful in healing; one is thankfulness, and the second is joy. It is really hard to have one without the other. A thankful heart is incredibly powerful. Jesus was surrounded by thousands of people in a rural area and did not even really have enough for Him and His disciples to eat. What did He do? He gave thanks to God for what He did have. And with that thanks, Jesus went on to feed several thousand people with what had begun as just five loaves of bread and two small fish. Not only that, after He had given it all away, He had twelve basketsful left over! More than He had started with and more than enough for what they needed. You may not think you have enough to face what confronts you, but if you give thanks for what you do have and let God use you, it will be more than enough. Joy is also a close cousin of praise and has miraculous healing properties. Interestingly enough, there is a word in Hebrew for medicine known as גֵּהָה, otherwise translated as *gehah*. It is used only one time in the Bible. It is not used to describe Lipitor or Prozac or penicillin; the verse says, "A cheerful heart is good medicine, but a crushed spirit dries up the bones" (Proverbs 17:22). A cheerful heart is literally like taking medicine, but so much better!

There really is an incredible verse that ties all this together, showing that it is God's desire for you to praise and worship Him. "Be joyful always; pray continually; give thanks in all circumstances, for this is God's will for you in Christ Jesus" (1 Thessalonians 5:16). How awesome is that? Joy, praise, and having a continually thankful heart is God's desire for you.

> Shout for joy to the Lord, all the earth. Worship the Lord with gladness; come before Him with joyful songs. Know that the Lord is God. It is He who made us, and we are His; we are

Edward W. Hellman, M.D.

His people, the sheep of His pasture. Enter His gates with thanksgiving and His courts with praise; give thanks to Him and praise His name. For the Lord is good and His love endures forever; His faithfulness continues through all generations. (Psalm 100)

Praise the Lord, O my soul; all my inmost being praise His Holy Name.
Praise the Lord, O my soul, and forget not all His benefits—who forgives all your sins and heals all your diseases, who redeems your life from the pit and crowns you with love and compassion, who satisfies your desires with good things so that your youth is renewed like the eagles.
The Lord works righteousness and justice for all the oppressed. He made known His ways to Moses, His deeds to the people of Israel; the Lord is compassionate and gracious, slow to anger, abounding in love.
He will not always accuse, nor will He harbor His anger forever; He does not treat us as our sins deserve or repay us according to our iniquities.
For as high as the heavens are above the earth, so great is His love for those who fear Him; as far as the east is from the west, so far has He removed our transgressions from us.
As a father has compassion on his children, so the Lord has compassion on those who fear Him; for He knows how we are formed, He remembers that we are dust.
As for man, his days are like grass, which flourishes like a flower in the field; the wind blows over it and it is gone, and its place remembers it no more.
But from everlasting to everlasting, the Lord's love is with those who fear Him, and His righteousness with their children's children—with those who keep His covenant and remember to obey His precepts.
The Lord has established His throne in heaven, and His kingdom rules over all.
Praise the Lord, you His angels, you mighty ones who do His bidding, who obey His word.
Praise the Lord, all His heavenly hosts, you His servants who do His will.
Praise the Lord, all His works everywhere in His dominion.
Praise the Lord, O my soul. (Psalm 103)

9) BE JESUS STRONG!

God is love. Whoever lives in love lives in God, and God in him. In this way, love is made complete among us so that we will have confidence on the Day of Judgment, because in this world we are like Him.
—1 John 4:17

Finally, be strong in the Lord and in His mighty power.
—Ephesians 6:10

It is quite an understatement to say that Jesus is amazing; in the book of John, Jesus is described as the Word: "In the beginning was the Word, and the word was with God, and the Word was God. He was with God in the beginning. Through Him all things were made; without Him nothing was made that has been made. In Him was life, and that life was the light of men. The light shines in darkness, but the darkness has not understood it" (John 1:1–5). Jesus is God, and through Him all things were made. He is holy, He is perfect, He is just. He is the way, the truth, and the light, He is all-powerful. He is also loving, and merciful, and knows even the number of hairs on our head, and knows even before a single sparrow falls to the ground. He is real and ever present. Jesus watches over our lives.

To me, Jesus is also incredibly tough and courageous. He was born to a poor family and became a carpenter, probably working until He started His ministry at the age of thirty. This was before the age of power tools and computers. He once walked into the crowded temple, took some cords, fashioned them into a whip, and drove the money changers forcefully out. Jesus confronted demons and threw them out. The Pharisees and Sadducees were constantly trying to trap Him and persecute Him, and yet He never backed down from the truth. Scripture predicted that His body would be so badly beaten that He would not be recognizable as a human, and yet He willingly chose to give up His life for ours. He took up our sicknesses and iniquities; we were healed by his wounds. He was pierced for our transgressions. Jesus was not passive, He was not a pushover; it says in scripture that Jesus came to destroy the work of the devil.

Edward W. Hellman, M.D.

Jesus was tough and determined in His mind-set. Are you tough? We are instructed, "Your attitude should be the same as Christ Jesus" (Philippians 5:11), and to be "imitators of Christ", and to "become as Christ." The Bible actually says, "But we have the mind of Christ Jesus" (1 Corinthians 12:27). We are told in scripture that in Jesus we are more than conquerors, and He that is in us is greater than he that is in this world. And so when we face a hardship, I think it is important to recognize our power and our authority that we have in Jesus and not to back down. Scripture recommends: "Finally, be strong in the Lord and His mighty power" (Ephesians 6:10). Understand that, if you are a believer, you are in Christ, and Christ is in you. When two people go into covenant relationship, one acquires access to the other's strengths. We are in covenant relationship with God. If you are coming up against some conflict, it is not you who should be afraid, or passive, or worried; it is Satan who should be worried.

I have listened to many sermons and read many books about the topic of why bad things happen to good people, and I have left these discussions with never a great peace about all I heard. In the end, I found only one book I was in complete agreement with; thankfully, it was the Bible. The Bible says, "The thief comes only to steal and kill and destroy; I have come so that you may have life, and have it to the full" (John 10:10), and, "'For I know the plans I have for you,' declares the Lord, 'plans to prosper you and not to harm you, plans to give you hope and a future'" (Jeremiah 29:11), and, "The One who is in you is greater than the one who is in world" (1 John 4:4). So when you face hardship, consider facing it as the empowered aggressor rather than as a passive victim. I like the term carpe diem. The popular translation for carpe diem is to "seize the day," but it is interesting to note that the term carpe literally means to "pluck" as in one picking a fruit. I picture the visual image of a person reaching down and forcefully taking hold of a situation or hardship and purposefully using it for God's glory. It very much describes an attitude a person can have as he or she goes throughout the day, overcoming and even taking advantage of any obstacle in the path. A person with a carpe diem attitude who faces hardship is not a passive victim; that person will overcome that hardship and even use it to his or her advantage. The opposite of this carpe diem attitude has also permeated some Christian and non-Christians alike. This is the belief that our lives are similar to objects floating down the current of a river and that nothing we say or do will have any significant impact on what happens in our lives. I strongly believe that what we do does have an enormous impact

Healing Grace

on our lives and the lives of others. The Bible actually says that if you resist the devil, he will flee from you, suggesting our attitude and response to things that happen to us can be very important. And how about this verse? "Whatever you bind on earth will be bound in heaven, and whatever you loose on earth will be loosed in heaven" (Matthew 16:19). That is a very real indication of our power on earth and the enormous impact we can have in how we live our lives. I have seen in my practice that the attitude a person has can have a rather dramatic effect on treatment outcomes. For example, two people can have the exact same hip fracture. One person never takes her eyes off Jesus, has faith she will overcome the hardship, and even uses the opportunity to minster to friends and family that come to her room to visit; that person is usually at home and recovering well from the injury very quickly. She is blessed and is a blessing to others. Another person with little faith has the exact same injury, but he develops a victim's mentality. They are difficult to mobilize and even after several days make little effort to work with therapy to even get out of the bed. He can start to get medical complications, and if he survives, his outcome may be drastically different from the other person's, even though they had the exact same injury. I submit to you it is a little like comparing a healthy tree to a diseased tree. A forest fire can scorch and burn the outside of a healthy tree, but in the end, it only makes the tree stronger. A forest fire can get on the inside of a diseased tree and bring it to the ground. The difference between a healthy tree and a sick tree is all based upon what is on the inside—as is the case with people.

Bethany Hamilton was a young woman pursuing a career in surfing when she was attacked by a shark. She lost most of one arm in the attack, and it looked as if her career was over. She not only has gone on to become a professional surfer, she became the subject for the movie *Soul Surfer* and has gone on to become an ambassador for people throughout the world, particularly those with disabilities, with her perseverant attitude and her bold stance for Christ. In the movie, Bethany tells reporters that, given the opportunity, she would not go back and change the events of that fateful day of the shark attack because it has given her such a platform to be a blessing and encouragement to others going through difficult times. By placing ourselves and our trust in Christ Jesus, we can more than overcome any hardship that confronts us and turn it into a way to glorify God. And knowing this, we can have this Christ-like attitude. Consider that the Bible says we are more than conquerors, that in Christ we can do all things, and that He who is in us is greater than he who is in this world. There was a Philistine giant named Goliath who was described in the Bible as being over nine feet tall. Saul and the seasoned army of Israel "were dismayed and terrified" at the sight of him. David was a young boy who saw the exact same giant, but his belief system and how he handled this hardship made the difference. The Bible says he "ran quickly toward the battle line to meet him." I submit to you he saw the problem in a different light than the army did. This is what he said: "I come against you in the name of the Lord Almighty … for the battle is the Lord's." He was "seizing" the battle in the Lord's name.

What is it that helps a mature Christian overcome hardship? At least three things come to mind. First is a strong, unswerving faith in Jesus. This faith is not contingent upon the person's surroundings. As we mentioned in a previous section of this book, these Christians have come to appreciate the importance of having Jesus be the strong foundation of their lives, and when a storm comes, they stand upon the rock and cannot be shaken. As scripture says, "My soul finds rest in God alone; my salvation comes from Him. He alone is my rock and my salvation; He is my fortress, I will never be shaken" (Psalm 62:1-2). Another characteristic of a mature Christian who faces hardship, particularly in the medical arena, is that this person takes responsibility for participating in the care of the condition. These Christians are not passive victims of the medical condition they have been diagnosed with; they are active participants in their treatment. And foremost in this acceptance of responsibility for being an active participant in their care is taking good spiritual and physical care of their own bodies. In the Old Testament, the tribe of Levi was responsible for both the physical and spiritual care of the temple, which held the very presence of the living God. What does the New Testament say? "For we are the temple of the living God" (2 Corinthians 6:16); "The kingdom of God does not come with our careful observation, nor will people say, 'here it is' or 'there it is,' because the kingdom of God is within you" (Luke 17:21); and, "Do you not know that your body is a temple of the Holy Spirit, who is in you, whom you have received from God?" (1 Corinthians 6:19). So where the Jewish nation had the tribe of Levi to care for the temple, I respectfully submit that under the New Covenant, that responsibility has been transferred to you. You are to take care of the temple and the kingdom of God that is within you. That really takes the thought process of taking care of your body and participating in your medical care to a whole new level. Make taking care

Healing Grace

of your body what it is meant to be, an act of service and worship to God. In this attitude, there is also an inherent understanding that nothing outside you can really hurt you. Jesus said that nothing outside you can make you unclean; it is the evil desires potentially within you that can make you unclean. This goes back to the idea of how important it is for you to take responsibility for yourself and your spiritual state. No one else can do it for you. I believe the Bible encourages us to do this in many places in scripture, including this verse about those who are obedient to God: "The Lord will make you the head and not the tail" (Deuteronomy 28:13).

The third characteristic that helps Christians overcome hardship is that they see everything that happens to them in their lives as an opportunity to serve God. Goliath was a massive soldier who evoked fear in the entire army of Israel; David saw it as an opportunity to serve God and ran aggressively toward battle. Paul was badly beaten and imprisoned and used it as an opportunity to witness to the prisoners, the warden, and his family; when an angel came to free him from prison at midnight, he found Paul singing hymns to God with all the prisoners listening. The Bible says that when we resist the devil, he will actually flee from us.

So to those facing physical hardship, I would encourage you to seize the opportunity to serve God. Be an active participant in the process and to take responsibility to care for the holy temple of God that is within you. See taking care of your body as an act of service and worship to God. Your body is a temple of God and is holy to Him. Other people can help you take care of this temple, but it is ultimately your responsibility. Take an active part in any medical care you are receiving, never take your eyes off Jesus, and take full responsibility in caring for your body. Seize any hardship you experience and treat it as an opportunity and a platform to serve Jesus. Have the attitude of Christ, who is with you always. He will never leave you or forsake you; He will empower you. If you are a believer, you are in Christ, and He is in you!

10) ASK

Ask and it will be given to you; seek and you will find; knock and the door will be opened to you. For everyone who asks receives; he who seeks finds; and to him who knocks, the door will be opened. Which of you, if his son asks for bread, will give him a stone? Or if he asks for a fish, will give him a snake? If you, then, though you are evil, know how to give good gifts to your children, how much more will your Father in heaven give good gifts to those who ask Him!
—Matthew 7:7-11

Ask and you will receive, and your joy will be complete.
—John 16:24

God wants to bless us, and He has blessed us. He also wants us to ask for things from Him; the Bible says it is so over and over. If God is all-powerful and all-knowing, and He knows we need something, why does He not just give it to us without asking? Well, sometimes He does, but when you ask God for something, a number of things happen. First, it leads us to be in relationship with Him. Asking for something is a form of praying to Him, and God does want us to pray to Him and be in relationship with Him. It is at times when we most desperately need something that our prayers are most fervent, and we open our hearts to Him. Many people who become saved as adults will have had a desperate need bring them to their knees to pray to God, and that is how their relationship with God started. Asking God for something also reestablishes the correct line of authority we should have in our lives. If we are in need, we should not turn to idols for help. Turning to God recognizes that God is the ultimate source of everything good in our lives; recognizing that is honoring to God. Asking God for something also develops faith in the believer. When I think of how great God is, among the things I remember is just how faithful He has been to me when I call on Him. That can only occur if we do call on Him.

So, I would certainly encourage anyone facing a hardship to ask for help from God. He wants you to turn to Him. I would also encourage you to ask with faith and trust, and also in patience. His way and His timing are perfect. There are some who are going through hardship who will receive a major spiritual breakthrough during the experience, all thanks to God's timing. It takes faith and trust to understand that God does want only good things for your life, as the scripture attests. And so, what you may see as a failure to have the prayer answered in the time and manner you wanted may in fact be the perfect answer. A good example of this is in the book of Daniel, which tells the story of Shadrach, Meshach, and Abednego. These three companions of Daniel refused to bow down and worship the false god that King Nebuchadnezzar of Babylon had created. The king was furious and threatened to throw them into a hot furnace. They replied, "If we are thrown into the blazing furnace, the God we serve is able to save us from it, and He will rescue us from your hand, O king. But even if He does not, we want you to know, O king, that we will not serve your gods or worship the image of gold you have set up" (Daniel 3:17-18). So they expressed faith that God would do the right thing, whether He saved them from the furnace or not. In the end, they were thrown into the furnace. The king looked into the furnace and saw a fourth person who looked like a "son of the gods" in the furnace with them. When they got out, they were completely unharmed. The truth is, God could have delivered them before they went into the furnace. But can you imagine how strong the faith of these men became after that incident? And what a testimony it must have been to the other Jewish people living in Babylon at that time?

There is another part of asking that I think is important, and that is that asking God for something involves us turning to Him. In other words, if we are trying to do things in our own strength, we may not be in relationship to God; we may have turned our backs to God. But asking God for something in prayer means, by definition, we have turned to Him for help. The prodigal son tried to sustain himself by his own efforts in a foreign land after he had rejected his father, but when he turned to his father and asked for help, his father had been looking for him and warmly embraced him as his son. There are times when we might get so caught up in the moment and all the crowds around us that even well-meaning people may keep us from asking God for help. You may be surrounded by friends, family, and even physicians who are telling you that you need to make an immediate decision about something, perhaps it is about your medical care; but don't let that keep you from turning to God first. There was a paralytic man who was brought by friends to Jesus, but the crowd was so great around Jesus that they could not get into the house where He was. They were determined to see Jesus, however, so they climbed onto the roof of the house and lowered the paralyzed man through the ceiling. They were rewarded when Jesus healed the man and forgave him of his sins. Zaccheus could not get to Jesus for the crowd, and he finally climbed a tree to see Him. He was rewarded with salvation! There was a blind beggar named Bartimaeus, crying out to Jesus in a crowd of His followers, and the crowd rebuked him and told him to be quiet. What did Bartimaeus do? He cried out to Jesus all the louder! And Jesus heard Bartimaeus, and He went over and healed him. Don't let "the crowd" keep you from Jesus, even if they seem more "religious" than you. We live in the New Covenant, and Jesus has offered to be continuously with us, so all it really takes on our part when we need help is simply to turn to Him and ask for it.

So scripture recommends over and over again that those going through hardship ask for help from Jesus. Another consideration I would like to add is this: if you are going to ask for something, ask for big things! There is an expression: feed a man a fish, and he eats for a day; teach him to fish, and he can eat for life. Ask for things that are really going to make a difference in your life and for the kingdom, and then have faith that Jesus will do it. God has said in scripture that He will give us things even greater than we can ask or imagine. It is just that the things we think we need and need immediately are not always the best things for us. This may even include immediately delivering you from the hardship you are going through right now, or delivering you from it in the exact manner you expect. A man might pray not to lose his job but may get laid off only to get an even better job. A person may go through sickness without an immediate cure, but come out with a stronger faith and even stronger immune system than she had before she entered the ordeal. A person may go through financial hardship but come out wiser and better off financially for the lessons he learned. Ultimately, even death is a lie; a Christian who dies goes to an incredible glory so great that not even our current minds can conceive the glory that awaits us in heaven. What are some big things to pray for? Wisdom, stronger faith, courage, a closer relationship with the Holy Spirit, boldness, and a stronger prayer life, just to name a few. Not to minimize your hardship, but know there may be so much more you can receive as a blessing from God than just Him getting you though a hardship as soon as possible. If you focus on serving God, the other things will take care of themselves. As scripture says, "But seek first His kingdom and His righteousness, and all these things will be given to you as well" (Matthew 6:33), and, "Delight yourself in the Lord and He will give you the desires of your heart" (Psalm 37:4).

There is another component of asking God for something that to me is an amazing thought, and it is incredibly encouraging and also empowering. God has already given us everything we need, so asking Him for something is not like many of us think. I submit to you that asking God for something is not the same as asking a person for something. When we ask a person for something, that person will consider your request and then must decide if they will honor it. Ultimately, they may or may not grant your request. Remember that God has already done all the work for us. He has already gained the victory for us. Asking God for something should not be viewed as a request but rather a calling forth of the very things we already have! Jesus has already died for our sin and has risen in victory, there is simply no more work that needs to be done. Asking God for something is a stepping out in faith, claiming things we have already been given. It is like carrying a checkbook around that gives you access to an account that is filled with incredible, limitless blessings. The covenant God has generously made with you allows you access to His "checking account" and all His limitless resources. Isn't that incredible? He is with you in a blood covenant where the two become one; everything that belongs to one belongs to the other. God has made a blood covenant with us through Jesus. So, for example, if you are asking for a healing in your life from something, you should not ask God to heal you like He is sitting up in heaven trying to decide whether or not to heal you; it should be done as a declaration and stepping out in faith that He has already healed you and claiming healing is your right as a member of a blood covenant with God and a coheir with Christ. The Bible says that by His stripes we have already been healed. It is all about claiming the promises you have already been given and stepping out in faith, not asking God for something and then wondering if He will do it. Consider the following verses: "'Have faith in God,' Jesus answered. 'I tell you the truth, if anyone says to this mountain, 'Go throw yourself into the sea,' and does not doubt in his heart but believes that what he says will happen, it will be done for him. Therefore I tell you, whatever you ask for in prayer, believe that you have received it, and it will be yours" (Mark 11:22-24). "If anyone of you lacks wisdom, he should ask God, who gives generously to all without finding fault, and it will be given to him. But when he asks, he must believe and not doubt, because he who doubts is like a wave of the sea, blown and tossed by the wind" (James 1:5-6). "Praise be to the God and Father of our Lord Jesus Christ, who has blessed us in the heavenly realms with every spiritual blessing in Christ" (Ephesians 1:3). "His divine power has given us everything we need for life and godliness through our knowledge of Him who called us by His own glory and goodness" (1 Peter 1:3). Scripture says, "Therefore I tell you, whatever you ask for in prayer, believe that you have received it, and it will be yours" (Mark 11:24), and, "If you believe, you will receive whatever you ask for in prayer" (Matthew 21:22). The Bible says, "Taste and see that the Lord is good; blessed is the man who takes refuge in Him" (Psalm 34:8). It does not say to ask God and maybe He will let you taste and see that He is good. Step out in faith and see that the promises God has given you and His grace and mercy are good. And the Bible says in doing this, you will be blessed! Even in asking for something as fundamental as faith itself, understand that it is a gift God has already given you and that in asking for it in the right way, you are claiming it rather than doubting whether or not you have it. The Bible says, "in accordance with the measure of faith God has given you" (Romans 13:3). God has already given you faith; claim it and use it! I believe something I have heard preachers say many times before—that faith can be like a muscle that, when used, can grow and become stronger, and when not used, can atrophy and weaken. The Bible says, "For everyone who has will be given more, and he will have an abundance. Whoever does not have, even what he has will be taken from him" (Matthew 25:29). That verse is from a story Jesus is telling in which a master gives his servants some money. Some invest it and make it grow, and one does not. I believe that parable has much to say about faith we have been given and how we use it.

Can I make a couple of examples of this principle that asking is more about stepping out in faith and declaring for something God has already given you than it is asking God to decide whether or not to give you something? The first is a football analogy. Have you ever seen a quarterback and wide receiver who work in complete harmony with each other? It is a pretty beautiful thing to watch. The wide receiver will run his route exactly as he has done over and over before; he opens his hands, and the quarterback delivers the ball exactly where it needs to go. The result is a perfect completion. They have established faith in each other and developed it until it is very strong. It took stepping out in faith and running the routes over and over for this relationship to become as strong as it is. In the end, the quarterback and the receiver have complete confidence and trust in each other, and the results are amazing. Another interesting part of this analogy is the defense. The defense will do everything it can do to disrupt this relationship; they will chase and try to harass both the quarterback and the receiver. A hostile crowd may even try to get involved. The devil would like to disrupt your relationship with God, your times when you step out in faith with Him, and the incredible things you could accomplish together. Just one example of this from our Christian past was a man name George Mueller, who lived in the 1800s. I submit to you that George Mueller and God had a very special relationship together. Mr. Mueller was initially financially a very poor man who was named pastor at a local church, but people noticed he did things a lot differently than other preachers of that time. Most preachers would be paid their income by renting pews in the church. The wealthy families would pay to have a prominent pew to sit in at church, and this would pay for the salary of their preacher. George Mueller did not do this; everyone could sit wherever they wanted, and he did not even take up a collection! This created quite a stir, and some people became quite upset. This turmoil meant George Mueller had to step out in faith to even have enough to eat for him and his wife, but he noted that God always provided, even sometimes at what seemed like the final hour. Later in his life, God told George to start an orphanage even though he had very little money, and he was obedient to this instruction. The orphanage grew to include multiple buildings and several hundred children. There would be times when there was not only no food in the pantry for the children but also no money to buy food. He would instruct the children to get ready for dinner like they normally would and sit down at the table and that God would provide, and God never failed them. He told of one time a bakery truck broke down in front of the orphanage, and the baker brought the truckload of bread into the orphanage for the children to eat just as they were sitting down at the table with no apparent food for them. Over and over, God would provide for those children, often at the last minute and often miraculously so; the children never went without. Mr. Mueller kept a detailed account of all the times God had provided for them and would often refer back to those times. Just like that receiver who runs his route and has faith that the quarterback will deliver the ball, Mr. Mueller had complete faith that God would provide. When George Mueller prayed and asked God to help his children, as he did often, I believe it was a stepping out in faith and a declaring that God would provide, in part based upon the many times that God had done so much for him before and an understanding of the covenant relationship they had.

There is an almost humorous event in the Bible about this very principle. Peter was arrested by King Herod and thrown in prison soon after James had been imprisoned and executed. Members of the early church met and prayed for his release. Miraculously, an angel went to the jail and released Peter and brought him to the very house where people were praying for him. Peter knocked on the door; a servant girl answered, and she went back into the house to tell the people that he had been released and was standing at the door. What happened? They did not believe her! Peter just kept on knocking, and ultimately the people came to the door and were astonished to see Peter. So, the very thing they were praying for happened, and they almost missed it! What if they had never opened the door? They might have not ever appreciated that their prayer had been answered! There is a short verse in the Old Testament that I think puts all that we have talked about in this section together, and it is this: "Open wide your mouth and I will fill it" (Psalm 81:10). This scripture uses the image of a baby bird being fed by its mother. You could write a whole book on this verse alone, but it covers the main topics we discussed when we ask God for something: total dependence on God, an expectation that God will provide, and an expectation for big things from God; He is more than able.

So, I believe the Bible advises those going through hardship to ask God for help, and He will help you, and to ask Him for really big things; He is more than capable. I also respectfully submit to you that asking God for something is not a matter of asking Him with the mind-set that He is up in heaven and trying to decide whether or not to help you; asking God for something is a matter of stepping out in faith and claiming the things He has already promised you based upon His covenant with you—truly tasting and seeing that the Lord is good!

> Let us then approach the throne of grace with confidence, so that we may receive mercy and find grace to help us in our time of need. (Hebrews 4:16)

11) CLIMB THE LADDER AND THEN HELP OTHERS UP: THE IMPORTANCE OF BEING ENCOURAGED YOURSELF AND ENCOURAGING OTHERS

> My soul is weary with sorrow; strengthen me according to your word.
>
> —Psalm 119:28

An amazing, incredible chain of events began long before we were ever born. "In the beginning was the Word, and the Word was with God, and the Word was God. He was with God in the beginning. Through Him all things were made; without Him nothing was made that has been made. In Him was life, and that life was the light of men. The light shines in the darkness, but the darkness has never understood it" (John 1:1–5). "In the beginning God created the heavens and the earth" (Genesis 1:1). God spoke, and light was created and was separated from darkness; God spoke, and the land, the sea, the sun, and the moon, and all the stars were created. God spoke, and all the animals on the earth were created. God spoke, and man and woman were created. God commissioned man to fill and subdue the earth and gave us plants to eat. God placed man and woman in the Garden of Eden to work it and take care of it. God instructed Adam and Eve not to eat from the tree of the knowledge of good and evil. Adam and Eve rejected God's instruction; they were evicted from the Garden of Eden.

At one point, God looked down upon the earth and noted that there was no one righteous, not even one. "All had sinned and fallen short of the glory of God." Over hundreds of years, God sent prophets to the people of Israel to warn and instruct them. Many were ignored and even killed. God breathed, and the scripture of the Old Testament was created, predicting the coming of the Messiah. This scripture had over three hundred predictions about the nature of the Messiah's coming, His life, and His death. For over four hundred years, scripture then stood silent, awaiting the predicted coming of the Messiah. Jesus came down to earth as God in the flesh. His life and death fulfilled the scripture that had been written hundreds of years earlier. He came as a servant; He was not recognized by many. He was despised and rejected, as predicted in the book of Isaiah. He willingly gave His life as atonement for our sins, redeeming us from sin and death. He rose again and gained victory over death.

After He died and rose again, He appeared to over five hundred people over a period of forty days. He instructed His disciples, and He promised the coming of the Holy Spirit to empower them after He left. He instructed them that He would return again in judgment. His disciples were filled with the Holy Spirit and were empowered to perform miraculous healings, signs, and wonders as they spread the news of Jesus throughout the world. God breathed, and the remainder of the scripture was created, predicting the return of Jesus and the salvation of the saints.

God created you, and He created me. We were formed in His image and likeness. We are fearfully and wonderfully made. God knows us so well that even the very hairs on our head are numbered. It is said, "For we are God's handiwork, created in Christ Jesus to do good works, which God prepared in advance for us to do" (Ephesians 2:10). Jesus has been described as the head of the church, and we have been described as His body. God has a plan for our lives. We are empowered in that we have Jesus sitting at the right hand of God the Father to intercede for us; we have the Holy Spirit within us to counsel and empower us; we have the Holy Scripture to guide and strengthen us; we have the authority and promises God has given us; we have the power of the church; we have powerful angels to serve us; and we have each other. We have the opportunities and the resources to do good and to serve God.

I respectfully submit to you that there is a chain of events that began before you were born and will continue after you leave this earth. You are a very important part of this process. As scripture says, "As God made Him who had no sin to be sin for us, so that in Him we might become the righteousness of God. As God's coworkers, we urge you not to receive God's grace in vain. For He says, 'In the time of my favor I heard you, and in the day of salvation I helped you.' I tell you, now is the time of God's favor; now is the day of salvation" (2 Corinthians 5:21-6:2). Is there any part of this scripture that would suggest you are not a critical part of God's plan?

So, what is God's plan for you and others that is so critical, particularly as it relates to someone going through a hardship? And how do you get from where you are now to being right in the center of that plan? It is all about Jesus, and more specifically, it is all about the love of Jesus. It is so incredibly critical and so often missed. One of the most incredible verses in the entire Bible to me is 1 Corinthians 13. It is often recited at weddings. But read it again, meditate on it, and realize how essential and potentially empowering this scripture is:

> And now I will show you the most excellent way.
>
> If I speak in the tongues of men and angels, but have not love, I am only a resounding gong or a clanging cymbal. If I have the gift of prophecy and can fathom all mysteries and all knowledge, and have a faith that can move mountains, but have not love, I am nothing. If I give all I possess to the poor and surrender my body to the flames, but have not love, I gain nothing.
>
> Love is patient, love is kind. It does not envy, it does not boast, it is not proud. It is not rude, it is not self-seeking, it is not easily angered, it keeps no record of wrongs. Love does not delight in evil but rejoices with the truth. It always protects, always trusts, always hopes, always perseveres.
>
> Love never fails. But where there are prophecies, they will cease; where there are tongues, they will be stilled; where there is knowledge, it will pass away. For we know in part and prophesy in part, but when perfection comes, the imperfect disappears. When I was a child, I talked like a child, I thought like a child, I reasoned like a child. When I became a man, I put childish ways behind me. Now we see but a poor reflection as in a mirror, then we shall see face to face. Now I know in part; then I shall know fully, even as I am fully known.
>
> And now these three things remain: faith, hope and love. But the greatest of these is love. (1 Corinthians 13)

Isn't that an amazing scripture? Without love, nothing else has any value or meaning. Love never fails! Borrowing the name of a Christian ministry, it is truly a "love worth finding," even a love that is critical to find! Jesus is the embodiment of that love. Scripture says that God is love. Can we find that kind of love? I have no doubt that when we are in heaven and do see Jesus face-to-face, we will know and understand and appreciate that love, but can we experience that now, while we are in the midst of this sinful, failing, discouraging world? I believe we can, and I believe that when we find it, we should help others on this path as well.

I have thought about it and prayed about the kind of love described in 1 Corinthians before—it just seems so critical to the life of a believer—but at times I have seemed so far from it. Recently, however, my eyes drifted down to the next verse after 1 Corinthians 13; consider what it says: "Follow the way of love and eagerly desire spiritual gifts, especially the gift of prophecy. For anyone who speaks in a tongue does not speak to men but to God. Indeed, no one understands him; he utters mysteries with his spirit. But everyone who prophecies speaks to men for their strengthening, encouragement, and comfort" (1 Corinthians 14:1-3). Wow! Think about it for a moment. How do we find the type of love described in 1 Corinthians 13? Well, the "way of love" described is to eagerly desire spiritual gifts (Jesus is described as the way, the truth, and the life). Prophecy is mentioned specifically but not as an end in and of itself, rather as a way to strengthen, encourage, and comfort others! This is the very yearning I have felt in my heart from the beginning. The desire of this book and my life is to be a source of encouragement and comfort for others, particularly those going through some form of physical hardship. That is the very reason I became an orthopedic and spinal surgeon.

So I have never heard a sermon or teaching on this, but I do feel like the way of love might be described as somewhat of a ladder with four steps, for both yourself and others. And I do believe it is critically important for every believer but particularly for those going through physical hardship. This "way of love" starts at the most basic level with encouragement. Encouragement for yourself to get you on the path, as well as encouragement for others. Encouragement can come for a simple kind word or gesture. It can come from an act of kindness. One very powerful way is a testimony. The Bible even says, "They overcame him by the blood of the Lamb and by the word of their testimony" (Revelation 12:11). The Bible says that God comforts us in our troubles so we may comfort others in their troubles. It says we are always to be prepared to give a reason for the hope we have to others. We should seek out people who need encouragement, particularly if we know they are going through things we have already gone through. I believe God wants us to do that. We should make sure we are encouraged ourselves, even to the point we should seek it out. Discouragement is a deadly poison. I believe very much in the scripture that says "a cheerful heart is good medicine, but a crushed spirit dries up the bones." It is literally true. If you feel yourself getting discouraged, fight it! Use scripture, use other believers, use the church. This book was written with the sole purpose of encouraging discouraged people; use the scriptures in this book! Be encouraged!

What is the next step in the ladder after encouragement? It is hope. There is a huge, life-transforming difference when someone goes from a state of discouragement to a state of hope. When someone is going through a hardship and they become encouraged, they start to get hope things can get better. Encouragement gets people out of a discouraged state into a state of hope. That is why another name for being discouraged is to be hopeless. Your encouragement of others, or your ability to become encouraged, has taken you to a much better state. As you get up on this ladder, you can look back at your formally discouraged state and see it for what it was—a lie. You can then make it a point to try to help and encourage others in a discouraged state, because you know what they are going through—and also how much better it is to have hope. The Bible says that hope in Jesus will never disappoint us. Consider this scripture about the importance of hope: "We who have fled to take hold of the hope offered to us may be greatly encouraged. We have this hope as an anchor for the soul, firm and secure" (Hebrews 6:19).

The third step in the ladder is faith. Faith is different and so much stronger than hope. The Bible says, "Now faith is being sure of what we hope for and certain of what we do not see. This is what the ancients were commended for" (Hebrews 11:1-2). Hope gives you the ability to see beyond your circumstances, but faith has the power to completely change your circumstances. Hope is being in a boat in the middle of a storm and believing you are nearing the shore; faith is standing on the shore. Just as being encouraged leads to hope, having hope in increasing measure leads to faith. The Bible says, "Faith is the substance of things hoped for." Faith is critical; the Bible says "without faith, it is impossible to please God." Jesus says that if we have faith even as small as a mustard seed, we have the power to literally move mountains; faith is extremely powerful. I believe faith is extremely important in healing as well. Jesus has said, "By your faith you are healed" and "By your faith it will be done to you." The maturity of a Christian can in large part be measured by the degree of faith he or she has.

What is the fourth and final step in this way of love? Love itself. As faith grows and matures and becomes stronger, what happens? A person with an absolute, unswerving, undaunted, unapologetic faith in the grace and mercy and power of God begins to live with what the world would describe as a reckless abandon: Noah built a massive boat on dry land, Abraham was prepared to sacrifice his son, Gideon sent home most of his soldiers before going into a battle with three hundred men against a vast army of 135,000, David attacked a fully armed giant with five stones and a slingshot—all based upon faith. Developing strong faith in God like that requires a strong, relational experience with Him and also unwavering obedience to Him. I submit to you that somewhere in the midst of having a daily dependence on God, a daily relationship with God, and an obedience to God, you will begin to experience through revelation that agape' love of God that the scripture talks about. And, if you take this into your heart, you will not only experience it for yourself, but you will be able to share it with others. Experiencing, knowing, and then sharing God will not only encourage others, it is the ultimate development of spiritual maturity. The beauty of it is that, at the final step of the pathway of love, it is Jesus Himself who is there giving it to you, and what you will come to realize is that it was yours all along. It was not earned by works; it was given to you because of the tremendous grace, mercy, and love of Jesus. As the Bible says, "For God did not give us a spirit of fear, but one of power, love, and self-discipline." The spiritual rewards of this love for the believer are bountiful and are meant for us now; these rewards will totally overwhelm anything that confronts you and rescue you from any situation you are in. Consider this promise in the Bible that comes with walking in love and obedience with God:

> You will be blessed in the city and blessed in the country. The fruit of your womb will be blessed, and the crops of your land and the young of your livestock—the calves of your herds and the lambs of your flocks.

Your basket and your kneading trough will be blessed.

> You will be blessed when you come in and blessed when you go out.
> The Lord will grant that the enemies who rise up against you will be defeated before you. They will come at you from one direction but flee from you in seven.
> The Lord will send a blessing on your barns and on everything you put your hand to. The Lord your God will bless you in the land He is giving you.

> The Lord will establish you as His holy people, as He promised you on oath, if you keep the commands of the Lord your God and walk in His ways. Then all the peoples on earth will see that you are called by the name of the Lord, and they will fear you. The Lord will grant you abundant prosperity—in the fruit of your womb, the young of your livestock, and the crops of your ground—in the land He swore to your forefathers to give you. The Lord will open the heavens, the storehouse of His bounty, to send rain on your land in season and to bless all the work of your hands. You will lend to many nations but will borrow from none. The Lord will make you the head and not the tail. If you pay attention to the commands of the Lord your God that I give you this day and carefully follow them, you will always be at the top, never at the bottom. (Deuteronomy 28 1:1–13).

A critic might point out that this was an Old Testament verse, and that there were approximately 613 commands in the Old Testament, and the only person who lived without sinning was Jesus. But we live under the New Covenant, and Jesus made it quite simple for us. What did he say? "Love the Lord your God with all your heart and with all your soul and with all your mind. This is the first and greatest commandment. And the second is like it: Love your neighbor as yourself. All the Law and the Prophets hang on these two commandments" (Matthew 22:37–40). So everything has ultimately come back to love; His love for us and demonstrating this love to others. Remember that much of it started with encouragement of self and others. Consider this verse, which instructs us to encourage others:

> Strengthen the feeble hands, steady the knees that give way, say to those with fearful hearts, "Be strong, do not fear; your God will come, He will come with vengeance, with divine retribution, He will come to save you." Then will the eyes of the blind be opened and the ears of the deaf be unstopped. Then will the lame leap like a deer, and the mute tongue shout for joy. Water will gush forth in the wilderness and streams in the desert. The burning sand will become a pool, the thirsty ground bubbling springs. In the haunts where jackals once lay, grass and reeds and papyrus will grow. And a highway will be there; it will be called the Way of Holiness. The unclean will not journey on it; it will be for those who walk in that Way; wicked fools will not go about on it. No lion will be there, nor will any

> ferocious beast get up on it; they will not be found there. But only the redeemed will walk there, and the ransomed of the Lord will return. They will enter Zion with singing; everlasting joy will crown their heads. Gladness and joy will overtake them, and sorrow and sighing will flee away. (Isaiah 35:3–10)

How much was accomplished in this verse by the simple encouragement of someone else!

As I complete this section, I would encourage you to take the pathway of love, to find it for yourself and to share it with others. It is truly the "most excellent way." It is the pathway to complete victory—a victory for you that was won for you and is available as a gift. Getting started simply begins with finding encouragement for yourself—through scripture, through appreciating and being thankful for God's gift of love; and then sharing it with others. This can be done by simple kind acts or words, or sharing your testimony. Encouragement leads to hope, which will not disappoint us. Hope leads to faith in God that will not fail us. Strong and tested, relational faith ultimately leads to a greater appreciation and internalization of God's love for you. Love conquers everything. Nothing can stand against God and His love. Claim your birthright! Consider this scripture and notice how it recommends that we encourage one another:

> Let us hold unswervingly to the hope we profess, for He who promised is faithful. And let us consider how we may spur one another on toward love and good deeds. Let us not give up meeting together, as some are in the habit of doing, but let us encourage one another—and all the more as you see the Day approaching. (Hebrews 10:23–25)

12) GO FORTH ... IN THE SPIRIT!

> All authority in heaven and on earth has been given to me. Therefore go and make disciples of all nations, baptizing them in the name of the Father and of the Son and of the Holy Spirit, and teaching them to obey everything I have commanded you. And surely I am with you always, to the very end of the age.
> —Matthew 28:18-20

Have you ever thought much about what Mary, the mother of Jesus, was like? Think for a moment about God the Father and how perfect and strong His love is. Think about how much He must really love His only son, Jesus. God created Mary, and He knew she would carry and give birth to Jesus and raise Him up as a child and adult to fulfill His destiny. God must have made Mary very special indeed. Mary is not really directly quoted a lot in the Bible, but she has a very short verse in John that I think is really profound. It is set in a very specific circumstance, but I think if you could take one instruction from the Bible and give it to a Christian, this is what it would be: "His mother said to the servants, 'Do whatever Jesus tells you.'" God the Father said something similar: "This is my Son, whom I love; with Him I am well pleased. Listen to Him!" (Matthew 17:5).

One of the things Jesus definitely said to His disciples was simply this: Go! He taught and trained up His disciples and then sent them out into the world. In Matthew 28, He tells us to go out into the world as well. Church was never meant to be a closed club where members come and are entertained and discuss the latest controversies in doctrine. The church body is to be the actual body of Christ, fulfilling the great commission in a powerful way. We all have a part in the body and are important; each one of us is a minister and is able to minister. For some, it may be answering the call to be a missionary in a foreign country. For others, going forth may mean reaching out to others in the community. Even a bedridden hospital patient has contact with people and can reach out and minister to them. I know I have been ministered to by patients whom I thought I was helping; I sometimes will leave a patient like that feeling they did more for me than I did for them.

But if this is a book that is supposed to be for people going through their own struggles, why would I be talking about going forth and ministering to other people? Well, if you believe in scripture and Jesus, take a moment and think about something you would really like to receive as a gift, no matter what it is. Then realize there is something that is so much better than that. You see, Jesus said, "It is more blessed to give than receive" (Acts 20:35). So if you give, trust in Jesus that it will actually be better than if you receive. Do you want to be great? Jesus said the greatest among you will be your servant. Do you want to be exalted? Jesus said that whoever humbles himself will be exalted. So, if you give, serve, and humble yourself, Jesus says you will be blessed, great, and exalted! There is only one place in the Bible where God asks us to test Him, and it is on the area of giving back (tithing) to God: "Bring the whole tithe into the storehouse, that there may be food in my house. Test me in this, says the Lord Almighty, and see if I will not throw open the floodgates of heaven and pour out so much blessing that you will not have room enough for it" (Malachi 3:9-11). In the New Testament, Jesus said whatever you do for the least of our brothers, you do for Him. Consider the first part of the famous scripture in John 3:16, "For God so loved the world *that He gave.*" All giving is not out of love. We can give for the wrong reasons, but I submit to you that true love always involves giving something of yourself. Watchman Nee once said, "One gains by losing self for others and not by hoarding for oneself." As scripture says, "A generous man will prosper; he who refreshes others will himself be refreshed" (Proverbs 11:25), and, "Whoever sows sparingly will also reap sparingly, and whoever sows generously will also reap generously" (2 Corinthians 9:6). Or, another favorite of mine from scripture that speaks more about the relationship between giving and healing: "Blessed is he who has regard for the weak; the Lord delivers him in times of trouble. The Lord will protect him and preserve his life; He will bless him in the land and not surrender him to the desire of his foes. The Lord will sustain him on his sickbed and restore him from his bed of illness" (Psalm 41:1-3), and, "You will be made rich in every way so that you can be generous on every occasion, and through us your generosity will result in thanksgiving to God" (2 Corinthians 9:11). Another way to look at this topic from the Old Testament is the subject of fasting. Many people would (and do) fast with the belief this practice will obtain something for themselves. But in Isaiah 58, God has said He prefers the fasting done this way: "Is not this the kind of fasting I have chosen: to loose the chains of injustice and untie the yoke, to set the oppressed free and break every yoke? Is it not to share your food with the hungry and to provide the poor wanderer with shelter—when you see the naked to clothe him, and not to turn away from your own flesh and blood? Then your light will break forth like the dawn, and your healing will quickly appear; then your righteousness will go before you and the glory of the Lord will be your rear guard. Then you will call and the Lord will answer. You will cry for help, and He will say 'Here am I'" (Isaiah 58:6-9). In other words, instead of fasting in attempt to try to receive something for yourself, fast by giving to others, and then you will actually receive much more. It is a long verse, but I would encourage you to read and meditate on the entire verse of Isaiah 58.

So what does it really mean to "go forth?" I submit to you that going forth is a state of mind, and that state of mind is that of a missionary. A missionary goes to a country that is not his own, understands the present times, and looks for opportunities to serve and share the love of Jesus with others. I submit to you that you do not have to leave the country to be a missionary. I have missionaries who work in my office. They repeatedly reach out and minister to the multitudes of patients with pain and suffering from orthopedic and spinal conditions who come through my office. They consistently go above and beyond what their job duty involves to provide encouragement and hope to my patients, and I am thankful for them. The same is true with so many people at the hospital that I work with as well. The medical field sometimes comes under fire in America, and sometimes rightly so, but I think if people could see the tremendous commitment of service that so many unspoken heroes have at the hospital, they would be truly inspired. I have spent so many times at midnight or 2:00 or 3:00 a.m. treating a trauma victim with a group of people displaying Christian love and commitment to excellence. I am proud and humbled to stand with them. Jesus wants us to look at things from a kingdom perspective. He says, "I tell you, open your eyes and look at the fields! They are ripe for harvest" (John 4:35).

Going forth is an act of obedience, and I believe God blesses obedience. I enjoy this scripture about those going on a pilgrimage to serve God; I love how it says they go from strength to strength. "Blessed are those whose strength is in you, who have set their hearts on pilgrimage. As they pass through the valley of Baca, they make it a place of springs; the autumn rains also cover it with pools. They go from strength to strength, till each appears before God in Zion" (Psalm 84:5-7). To read scripture and listen to sermons can allow you to know about God, but to walk in obedience to God by going forth allows you to actually know God. As the Bible says, "If anyone would come after me, he must deny himself and take up his cross daily and follow me" (Luke 9:23). I will say also that going forth in your own strength is probably not a good idea. For victory, it is not so much to simply go forth but rather to go forth walking with the Holy Spirit and His power. The Bible tells one story about some people who simply "went forth" but really in their own strength. They were known as the "seven sons of Sceva," who was a Jewish high priest. The sons would go and try to cast out demons in the name of Jesus, but they had no relationship with Him or the Holy Spirit. They had simply heard that the apostles were doing it and thought they could do it as well, almost like it was some sort of parlor trick. What happened? The demons jumped on them, attacked them, and sent them running from the house naked and bleeding!

If I could ask for one thing in my life (and I have), my family, and even the church in general, it would be to walk with the Holy Spirit more and more, to be completely in step with Him and to be led by Him. I think we all need this. It is really critical to our lives here on earth. The Bible says, "So, I say, live by the Spirit, and you will not gratify the desires of the sinful nature. For the sinful nature desires what is contrary to the Spirit, and the Spirit what is contrary to the sinful nature. They are in conflict with each other, so that you do not do what you want. But if you are led by the Spirit, you are not under law. The acts of the sinful nature are obvious: sexual immorality, impurity, and debauchery; idolatry and witchcraft; hatred, discord, jealousy, fits of rage, selfish ambition, dissensions, factions and envy; drunkenness, orgies and the like. I warn you, as I did before, that those who live like this will not inherit the kingdom of God. But the fruit of the Spirit is love, joy, peace, patience, kindness, goodness, and self-control. Against such things there is no law. Those who belong to Christ Jesus have crucified the sinful nature with its passions and desires. Since we live by the Spirit, let us keep in step with the Spirit. Let us not become conceited, provoking and envying each other" (Galatians 5:16-26). If each of us walked more in step with the Spirit, it would satisfy all our other needs as well. As scripture says, "But seek first His kingdom and His righteousness, and all these things will be given to you as well" (Matthew 6:33).

So, if this entire book was just one sentence, I would simply tell anyone going through any hardship whatsoever to go forth in the Spirit. It really is that simple—not necessarily easy but simple. If you walk in the Spirit, you will demonstrate the fruits of the Spirit, which are love, joy, peace, patience, kindness, goodness, and self-control. Love conquers everything. Nothing can stand against love. How can we walk in step with the Spirit? First of all, we can ask. Jesus said that He sits at the right hand of the Father, and whatever we ask for in His name He will give us. I think God even wants us to ask for this. In scripture, which is written by God, He says, "Which of you fathers, if your son asks for a fish, will give him a snake instead? Or if he asks for an egg, will give him a scorpion? If you then, though you are evil, know how to give good gifts to your children, how much more will your Father in heaven give the Holy Spirit to those who ask Him?" (Luke 11:11-13). He wants us to ask for the Spirit! Think about it. If God knows you are going to face many trials in your life on earth, I think He would want you to have the Holy Spirit with us to help us to overcome them. He knows you might have a battle on your hands, but He is offering to send you out into it with a weapon—and not a water pistol, but a bazooka! The Holy Spirit is the ultimate bodyguard.

Asking and receiving the Spirit is not the same as walking in the Spirit. You can have the Spirit inside you and not walk with it. The Bible warns us, "Do not quench the Spirit" (1 Thessalonians 5:19), and, "Do not grieve the Holy Spirit of God" (Ephesians 4:30). Put another way, "Those who cling to worthless idols forfeit the grace that could be theirs" (Jonah 2:8). "The Spirit is willing, but the body is weak" (Matthew 26:41). Those verses suggest you have some input about whether or not you are going to walk in the Spirit, and I submit to you it is based upon a daily decision you must make to do so. You must decide whether you are going to walk in the Spirit today. The Spirit will not force you to do so. Understand that the world and the Spirit are at complete war with each other, and so if you are going to serve the world, you will not be walking in step with the Spirit. As Joshua said to the people of Israel, "But as for me and my household, we will serve the Lord" (Joshua 24:15). Joshua was entering a world of idolatry and foreign gods and making a conscious decision to follow God. Joshua realized he could not serve the foreign gods and the one true God; as the Bible says, "for the Lord you God, who is among you, is a jealous God" (Deuteronomy 6:15). Likewise, we cannot serve the idols of this world—money, fame, job promotion, even religion—and serve our God with all our heart. We must make a choice about whom we are going to serve. As the Bible says, "Do not be deceived: God cannot be mocked. A man reaps what he sows. The one who sows to please his sinful nature, from that nature will reap destruction; the one who sows to please the Spirit, from the Spirit will reap eternal life. Let us not become weary in doing good, for at the proper time we will reap a harvest if we do not give up. Therefore, as we have the opportunity, let us do good to all people" (Galatians 5:7-10). One way to walk in step with the Holy Spirit is to praise Jesus. The Bible says, "no one can say 'Jesus is Lord,' except by the Holy Spirit" (1 Corinthians 12:3). The Bible also talks about other ways to live in unity with the Spirit: "I urge you to live a life worthy of the calling you have received. Be completely humble and gentle; be patient, bearing with one another in love. Make every effort to keep the unity of the Spirit through the bond of peace. There is one body and one Spirit—just as you were called to one hope when you were called—one Lord, one faith, one baptism, one God and Father of all, who is over all and through all and in all" (Ephesians 4:1-6).

Ultimately, I do think walking with the Spirit all comes down to love. As Jesus said, "Love the Lord your God with all your heart and with all your soul and with all your strength and with all your mind" (Luke 10:27). Walking in step with the Spirit means walking in love with the Spirit and putting everything else aside. "Be imitators of God, therefore, as dearly loved children and live a life of love, just as Christ loved us and gave Himself up for us as a fragrant offering and sacrifice to God" (Ephesians 5:1-2). Do you love God enough to put everything else aside to follow Him and be obedient to Him? If you can do this, nothing can ever stop you. Walking in the Holy Spirit is literally the game-changer for living in victory while we are still on earth. Imagine the Spirit of God within you counseling you and empowering you! Think about the apostles. They had spent three to four years with Jesus, seeing Him perform miracles and learning from Him. And yet after He died, they become discouraged and frightened, even to the point where some of them had returned to their jobs as fisherman and would meet hiding in a locked upper room for fear of the Jews. But when the Holy Spirit came upon them, they became filled with power and boldness and began demonstrating miracles of healing and wonders and spread the word of Jesus throughout the world. Heaven awaits the believer, and I believe it will be amazing, but the Holy Spirit lives within a believer here and now, and walking in step with Him means complete and total victory right now! And to what end is all this?

> To prepare God's people for works of service, so that the body of Christ may be built up until we all reach unity in the faith and in the knowledge of the Son of God and become mature, attaining to the whole measure of the fullness of Christ. Then we will no longer be infants, tossed back and forth by the waves,

> and blown here and there by every wind of teaching and by the cunning and craftiness of men in their deceitful scheming. Instead, speaking the truth in love, we will in all things grow up into Him who is the Head, that is Christ. From Him the whole body, joined and held together by every supporting ligament, grows and builds itself up in love, as each part does its work. (Ephesians 4:12–16)

Remember, too, that the Holy Spirit is a "seal" of our covenant with God. Through this covenant, incredibly, we have access to everything that is God's. Our part in that covenant is to realize that, as a covenant partner with God, everything that is a part of our lives needs to be turned over to God as well. Not to fulfill our role in being part of this blood covenant will "grieve the Spirit," one of the things the Bible warns us not to do.

Ultimately, everything in Christianity has begun and ended with God, His love, and His grace. As the Bible says quite simply, "The only thing that counts is faith expressing itself through love" (Galatians 5:6). Jesus said that loving God with all your heart, soul, strength, and mind was the first and greatest commandment. Do you love God enough to walk in obedience to Him and to serve Him totally, turning every aspect of your life over to Him? How appropriate it is that scripture says the very nature of God is love. When you find God, are obedient to Him, and turn your entire life over to Him, you will find true love. When you find it, you will realize it was yours all along; it was a gift from the tremendous grace and mercy of God, not something you need to, or are even able to, earn by your works. For those going through hardship, this is victory; for love conquers everything.

For those going through hardship, love God with everything that is in you. Die to yourself and, most importantly, receive the love He has given you. Serve Him wholeheartedly. Walk in step with the Spirit, who is the very seal of the blood covenant we have with God, and you will have total victory right now for your life; that is your gift and your birthright. As scripture says, "Whoever pursues righteousness and love finds life, prosperity and honor" (Proverbs 21:21). You can do it! Receive what has been put aside for you! God wants you to have it and for you to walk in victory right now!!

> Be on your guard; stand firm in the faith; be men of courage; be strong. Do everything in love. (1 Corinthians 16:13–14)

Edward W. Hellman, M.D.

Thank you for taking the time to read this book! My prayer is that in ever-increasing measures you will come to know God and be filled with His goodness and blessings! Please remember that even on a day when you are going through something that is particularly hard, the God who made the heavens and the earth and everything in it loves you and cares for you and wants you to be encouraged and live in victory. He has given you His precious Son, Jesus, who has paid for your sin and taken your sickness upon Himself that you may be healed.

He loves you that much!

Thank you again,
Edward W. Hellman, M.D.

> I pray that out of His glorious riches He may strengthen you with power through His Spirit in your inner being, so that Christ may dwell in your hearts through faith. And I pray that you, being rooted and established in love, may have power, together with all the saints, to grasp how wide and long and high and deep is the love of Christ, and to know this love that

surpasses knowledge—that you may be filled to the measure of all fullness of God.

Now to Him who is able to do immeasurably more than all we ask or imagine, according to His power that is at work within us, to Him be the glory in the church and in Christ Jesus throughout all generations, for ever and ever! Amen.
—Ephesians 3:16-21

May the Lord make your love increase and overflow for each other and for everyone else, just as ours does for you. May He strengthen your hearts so that you will be blameless and holy in the presence of our God and Father when our Lord Jesus Christ comes with all His holy ones.
—1 Thessalonians 3:12-13

If you have any comments, questions, or would like to share your testimony about what God is doing in your life please visit us at our website at www.healinggracethedevotional.com

Edwards Brothers Malloy
Thorofare, NJ USA
April 13, 2016